MONEY COMES 2 MONEY

After the Rampage of Franken-Germ

Man of Letters
Jabbar

ISBN 978-1-63874-670-6 (paperback)
ISBN 978-1-63874-671-3 (digital)

Christian Faith Publishing, Inc.
832 Park Avenue
Meadville, PA 16335
www.christianfaithpublishing.com

Printed in the United States of America

Contents

Let's us pray.

Father God, in the mighty name of Jesus, we come before you today to thank you that we were able to see another day. Father God, in the name of Jesus, we pray, decree, declare, and plead the blood of Jesus over this conversation that the devil and his imps would not hear or hamper the abundance of my heart. Lord Jesus, thank you for the new job, contract, and being accepted into the school of my choice. We thank you for giving us favor that surrounds us like a shield. In Jesus's name we pray, amen.

Acknowledgments

After the Sabbath Day service, the Holy Spirit came upon me like the time Samson had to fight, but this was for the growling in my stomach that needed to be tamed. Just resting on me to comfort me according to scriptures that states, "Jesus left the earth for the Comforter," a.k.a. the Holy Spirit to comfort us. And I totally embraced the Holy Spirit and your guidance even when it comes to eating out on the town.

I recall in law studies when the judge and law professor told us, "Never eat at a place that you can't sue." And I carry that plus all the spots that have slamming food where the chef will come out to take your order and cook it too. For the Lord Jesus has truly blessed this Greek Community for years and when I come here even with a client. The chef always comes out to serve my company and me. That's better than a waiter, yet I will leave the waiter a tip. That's shows appreciation, and they remember you. Trust me.

The food is always great and worth the travel and funds. It is a place where I had sealed my first three contracts for my new business and an answer to prayer. God knows that I have numerous eating spots to seal deals and just to forget about your diet spots too. The original name of this book was *The Seven P's of Prosperity*, which I thought about while traveling to the best Greek restaurant in Queens, Alidi A-da. The first book from your fellow New Yorker to brace yourself due to all the financial spending. In college, they taught us a few things on money, and life threw us a chance to earn more.

This is the same restaurant that fed me all throughout my first year in LaQuardia Community College, where majored in Paralegal Studies and Business Administration as a full-time student working three jobs and raising a newborn with the help from the mother of our child, aunts, and both grandmothers. Yes, it was hard at that time, but God made a way and I winded up working the perfect internship, which rolled into a job with a duration of six years. It was plenty of time to get paid, stack some, finish college, pursue a higher degree, and live a prosperous life going forward. Many people of whom I had the pleasure to discuss various ways of stacking and stashing can help all of us, not just for a short time but for the long haul. Many of them always realize the one factor of having at least one thousand dollars on hand. They apply every powerhouse of discipline after my two-hour discussion on finances. Follow me on my Twitter, for I will post the list of the items that will not be in stores from July up until early October. I pray that I am wrong. See, when Abraham had been blessed by God for his continuance of faith, he was so blessed that Isaac, Father of the Jews, and Ishmael, Father of the Arabs, both have been blessed. Later on in history, God's love was imparted by him sharing his only begotten Son that whosoever believeth on him shall not perish, but have everlasting life (John 3:16).

Remember, a budget is like shoes; they only work when you put them to work and be comfortable to withstand the approaching rough terrain. Well, your wallet is like shoes taking a beating when too many debts are around too. This game plan is for you to make it happen and kill your bills and live comfortable and within your means. Also, don't make new bills! The best advice that we all need to keep in mind is that there are moments and windows of opportunity where God sends someone through to help you get a great handle on your finances, and it works when we seriously apply the new great and anointed advice that propels us going forward and helps not just the body of Christ, but all those who need guidance outside of social media and their personal and secondary circles of life. No man or woman or child is an island unto thine self.

Introduction

This very book is written for those that come into money and out of the rut of being poor, impoverished, and living in the land of lack which affects the lives of various cultures of people that I have discussed a wealth of information not limited to *budgets* .

When budgeting, there are examples: for food stamps via Supplemental Nutrition Assistance Program (SNAP), public assistance (cash), being paid weekly, every two weeks, and even being paid once a month and being paid on Social Security disability insurance plus pensions too. And to *stash* some to invest and get paid more with converting bad debt via liability into wealth where you can eat in the future.

Budgets are the essential things that we all need to live and work by that allows us to have funds for virtually anything that we can afford without going into credit cards and borrowing money from others. It keeps us grounded and out of the stress zone of not having enough to do whatever we need to do. Always keep in mind that a budget can help anyone, even when you have a little money or get food stamps too . A budget works to keep your house, life, and all the things you care about in place going forward and allows you to store, stack, invest, and accumulate more than enough funds to be okay during anytime the nation's economy decides to take a turn for the worst; you will be okay. You can develop a method to live and move around like the Romans, not be a target within hard times, and border with safety too.

Yes, budgets do work and require discipline. Plus, there are many avenues and techniques that will allow you to excel in stacking and stashing, even for a little jump start. These tools that I share with you are some neat pointers that bring you from the past of debt and lack, into a life where you can breathe again and be stress-free while living on earth. For it is many people's desire to want the best in life for themselves, their families, and their friends as well. However, there needs to be some rules in place when it comes down to money. Like a woman had told a friend that I know, "You are going to need a new safe." That is what's supposed to happen after reading this book and fully work on the plan laid out for you to achieve, for without achievement there can be no stress-less life in the world of finance. So for all those who have new jobs, new positions, new contracts, and formed new partners or made partner to a firm/company, and to those who are working in the field of their studies, I tip my hat off to you! For those who are making it happen against all odds and use their haters as their footstool, God bless you and all that you do. For it is people like you that are relentless and are the examples of what to do and how to get it done without nonsense and lunacy. May God bless you and the works of your hands and enjoy the love provided to you that will make a difference in your life, family, and finances. For if it's not going correctly, then ask that man upstairs, "What am I doing wrong, or what needs to be done better?" God will do it for you. Just don't get mad at the answer when it comes. Okay?

DISCLAIMER: I am not a licensed financial expert. However, these examples are to help you go into stashing for you and whatever ventures that may come about for you to profit at or just to let it grow. It is one of the best ways of stashing and not having the thirsty, or lack of money look, and for such other reasons, *you need to have a stash*! Well, for all things to work out well, one must remember not to take any of the examples given out of context, because the plans can work for you. The plans work for you to have rent paid into the future, stash, and for you to have funding for that vacation that you always wanted. Instead of using your tax refund to pay bills, it can be used to invest some and have a vacation with the rest or just sit and relax while your investments pay off. The budgets presented within work especially for those who have relaxed rent or low mortgage or maintenance for (condos or coops), which can work for virtually anyone in higher rent conditions. But for those who want to *stack cash* and be all right going forward, this book is for you so you will not have a thirsty look on your face, like your life is cash-starved, once other people or your family and friends pull out money to count, give, or just to arrange it before putting it away. You will not have the look on your face like there is a *cash drought in your life*, and that's what the examples in this book will keep you saturated with cash on-hand despite the issues of the Franken Germ that's running around the globe.

And once again, I would like to thank you for purchasing this book. Enjoy!

Progress

The purpose of this book is to give you some financial tactical tools that work and so you will keep loot in your pocket for whenever you have to do something and whenever you want to just pack up and say, "I'm out!" It all matters how you stack and stash correctly and with discipline. After speaking with quite many people about stashing, God laid in my heart that this project had to come forth. This book was supposed to be the first before *Really???* came out to share with many on stashing money and not being suckered into messing with digital money by itself, have some silver and gold to be able to buy food, security for yourself and family, and live abundantly. Make serious changes that breed investments, and don't look desperate because you do not have enough or you keep saying that you are broke. Because if you're reading this book in the USA you will stop saying that you're broke. Also, because EMDs and EMPs, along with other electronic money transfers, are competing with each other and is leaving an opening in the new market to move cash out as quickly as long as it's been here. Thanks to HR 4827, "Killing of the Dollar" in 2014 came in, and it seems harder to stash due to debt. The retirement of the dollar is not going to happen yet because so many things are tied to the American dollar system. And this is why it is better to have silver, gold, and a variety of liquid assets plus hard assets to make a diverse portfolio. Stocks, Forex, Commodities, Futures are good on paper and materialism, but it's better to stay in your lane and work with what's attainable and keep your eyes on when things are fully better to make those leaps into those markets.

When one stashes funds to the side, they are actually setting something to the side that is scriptural. It's the same thing when you open a savings or escrow account. But this is different and more serious than you ever can imagine.

The techniques therein shall help you to have a stash and be able to pay off all your bills in such a way that you would be shocked and happy at the same time all because you took the paths of knowledge and discipline to move forward aggressively while maintaining a life that is stress-free. In our current tax cuts, I will suggest that you buy a silver coin or bullion every time a small bill is paid off. Keep in mind that you are starting off small. While paying one particular bill off, one may put a few singles or dollar bills to the side. Guess what? It's a start. I started my stash putting $7, $10, and $25 dollars in place for three separate stashes. See, when you have it in the stash, you don't have to spend it.

Do I Get a Return on My Stash?

Yes, it's called *peace within thy borders* (Psalm 122:7) and all the provisions of Deuteronomy 28:1–14 and Matthew 6:38 because money circulates back to the point of origin when you give. It gains the velocity of bringing more back with it. Like when a person gets saved and delivered from habitual sins, when he or she backslides, they invite the original habitual demons back and seven more return with guest. Well, money is somewhat like this analogy that when we give to nonprofit organizations we get a tax write-off, and Matthew 6:38 says, *"Give and it shall be given unto you."* This is called *point of circulation.* From the point of origin, back to you with interest, that is the gift of sowing and reaping. Remember that, because it's how other companies are reaping what they sowed; you purchasing their products. Some did it on credit, others with debit, others used a catalog order, a few did it with money orders, and honestly, that keeps you out of debt too. But it's good to pay with cash or a cash card like American Express Serve card. It's non-chip transactions process quicker than chipped transactions, and you are not charged a fee for using their services online and other places. It is a valuable tool to have and load money on it to handle light transactions, and most of all, when places don't accept your card, that's your cue to say to yourself, "This is where I keep my money and keep it moving." That's a financial rejection, and by leaving with that mind-set, you are on your way to seeing the fruits of your labor.

When we circulate money into giving, we are initiating a valuable law called sowing. The end product is reaping, not karma. The objective of sowing is to share in the partaking of your wealth, which came from either a volume of resources that you only know where and what you have that God has blessed you with and your moving in obedience that brings the tools of favor, blessings, and peace. Plus, you're bulletproofing your residence from economic famine and a wide spread of other unwarranted and needless issues.

Deal Maker

Most people are so far in debt that this advice that I specifically share is exactly necessary to jump on, and it starts from the first seed sown, until the first bill was paid and the purchase of one silver coin or gold (based on your dough flow) was made. All these above-mentioned has worked, and well, another thing, if you don't have a lockbox or safe, it's wise to invest in one. *Lock your credit cards up!* This is the *biggest deal maker that you can do for yourself* if you have no self-control. And even if you do, *lock those cards up*! There is no need to walk around with them, and it's cool to have them out of your wallet or purse; it may take some time to get used to, but the rewards are *great*! That's the best advice that I give many people and they apply to their lives and tax time. They reap the rewards of going on vacations or staycations.

Also, sowing a seed of some loot to help is activating a heavenly blessing as long as you keep your mouth shut—no advertising, no social media look-what-I-did moment. Don't you dare do that because the funds you shared out were not from the heart; they were to get people who are selfish or as selfish as you to be impressed about your act of alleged "kindness" or a public relations campaign moment. When it wasn't about kindness, it was just trying to look good and get that infamous pat on the back or likes. Now, there are those who have done something close to stashing and having peace. There are examples of public policy changes where kindness is a tool to soften or ease tense relations. For example, the police who gave a homeless man some socks. Another was either a first responder or regular Joe/Jane who has given anything from blankets, clothing, food, water, and some aspects of temporary shelter (if we kicked the UN headquarters out of NYC, my opinion solely). We can adequately provide the homeless, veterans, and others housing instead of a clubhouse on the east side of Manhattan. The other is to make *real affordable housing* for those who have or seem to have decent [1]affordable [2]housing.

That's only if we really care to take action and do something more than just talk—doing something that requires the level of help to help our own here on US soil. But that is a topic for real proactive and positive outreach, not for now.

The progress of giving is the total capacity of knowing that eventually you will receive more than what your output is while killing your liability debt, like credit cards and mortgage. (When the property is not paying you, it's a liability. Example: renting an apartment or parking space in the driveway will bring you income, yet you don't have to do it.). You may hear people making $100,000 a year with $3,000 in savings and $45,000 in debt is bananas. One person who makes $450,000 a year owes a note on two houses and bought a car just like his supervisor yet complains about being broke, even if he gets paid once a month. Lastly, the one person who clears $700,000 owes student loans but has no savings and absolutely has nothing in the stash at all. These are examples of people who make money and recklessly yell out that they are broke. Many people would love to trade places with them *anytime*! These are some of the people in life that have insane debt and totally cash poor. Their families are all around; some reason out, others ask why. But if you're hearing this in your life travels, then imagining it is wild as well.

There has been a volume of people who died in the family, and I will discuss this later on. People or loved ones have passed away and left individuals as their beneficiaries. My condolences to you and your family. However, the business portion of this is taxes, budgets, and also stash so that you can breathe. Plus, we all grieve differently,

---

1 Affordable housing (if it exists) is not rent at $1,200 a month. It's truly $400 for a studio, $500 for one-bedroom (with a terrace or balcony, $650), $800 for a two-bedroom (with a terrace, $900 or $1,000), $1,200 for a three-bedroom (with a terrace, $1,500), and $1,600 for a four-bedroom (with a terrace, $2,000).

2 It's not like a person lives in a MayTag box and eats his meals from a hub cap. As long as we don't know what you ate last night, we can presume that you have a stable roof over your head.

and this topic will be discussed later on after the retirement—Social Security budgets.

The past never sees the future unless we curtail the things in our present and make way for the better days ahead.

Prior

In life, there are processes we all have to face. Some call it prepping, others call it preparing, and few just have a thought and act on this notion. We obtain some level of insight or foreknowledge to aid us in making informed decisions that will reap benefits that we can share the rewards with those we love or continue to feed the stash. This insight allows many to press on and step into the area of anticipation of reaping for all the times you sowed and now it comes the time to reap. This anticipation we can define as faith or hope. "For faith is the substance of things hoped for and it is the evidence of things received" (Hebrews 11:1).

Since the time of birth until we are able to take care of ourselves, there is a process all mankind goes through. We unknowingly anticipate that in our world today someone is going to care for us, nurture us, and provide all the necessary tools needed to achieve the expectation of growing. As a child grows, there is reliance upon the caregiver to feed, clothe, and protect us from danger. It is the beginning environment that provides us a sense of security and shelter that is necessary for all human beings. Also, everything you read from this point on basically collaborates with "Peace be within thy walls, and prosperity within thy palaces" (Psalm 122:7) and allows you to experience the "LORD willt bless [you]; with favour wilt thou compass surround [you] as with a shield" (Psalm 5:12). All interact for the best outcome, which satisfies your life going forward in alignment with "Thoughts of peace, and not of evil, to give you an expected end" (Jeremiah 29:11), thus maintaining the *blessing*. This is avoiding being *broke*, which is a *sin* and *crime* against you and your household that affects your community and all that need to coexist onward.

That's why in this chapter; it is essential that we have to be mindful of the following:

People. They can be in one's life that would show you how to flourish or complete your goals, or they can be a problem for you and your goals going forward.

Places. This can be where you grew up or went to school at. It includes people as well. Also, it helps to understand diversity on who discusses wealth or can construct legit streams of wealth whether it be selling socks, gloves, hats, and underwear just to flip the proceeds. It all counts to meeting all and any financial goals that you have. Remember, not all people are saving for tomorrow, a vacation, or a trip, especially that it may cost a fortune versus where they reside at currently. This was probably arranged in the heavens before you prayed for a new place of residence that satisfies all your needs and not just part of your needs.

Things. Keeping a budget allows you to evaluate your vices and other bad habits not calculated into your budget. Most people fail to be honest here and with themselves. *You must be honest here*, because when a person just says they smoke two packs a week and they smoke more than the two packs, then the truth is told when the results come forth. Truth be told, they drink and smoke four packs, and $75 is 420 a week. I saved a lot of money when I was healed from smoking cigarettes, and I can tell you, there is a ton of revenue to do things with than figuring things out. Honesty is the key to having a successful and powerful budget and having a great stash too!

Damaged Goods

This term can be used for a number of different people in life, but it seriously applies to those that have lacked to remember "store up for yourselves treasure in heaven…for where your treasure is, there your heart will be also." Matthew 6:20–21 (NIV) shows us that damaged goods are the people who have labelled themselves a problem and have a sickness of insecurities and other levels of depression which are in their heads, in their hearts, and in their lives. These people move with the strength of desperation. The thoughts of obtaining what they want rather than what they need to get things right is their objective being that their entire life depends on getting over the troubled moment so they can go back to not establishing anything for tomorrow or later in life. It is shameful and keeps them on the wheel of running around aimlessly. Now this is one type of people who use others to save their loot and energy with senseless drama that is so convoluted, which breeds non-growth and all loot spent is being spent on useless nonprofitable things and events and invites lack and no real value or return on anything or events that they attend. What kind of person is this that wandered into your life? Drama, stress, and an unwanted distraction to keep your mind on your money, which that person wants you to spend like a rock star. Sadly, the rush to drama, senseless actions, and reckless with loot is a recipe for exiting, for this distraction is going to derail you. When you're on your grind to accomplishing goals and aspirations in life, you don't play lazy or with confusion around you. Now, there will be people that are lazy and who milk the government and don't care what goes on. They continue to milk the land until it all stops. When the land stops giving milk, being lazy and dependent upon society has them in peril. Make no mistake, there are people who need assistance from the government; however, there are those who milk the system. They're stunting their growth. Had they been exposed to other options, then their talents could've made them a fortune.

Yet the anvil of lack of knowledge and poverty robs people of potential, and debt can make people become depressed and use all types of substances instead of using their funds wisely. Not everyone who uses drugs or drinks has bad financial issues. They may have a few issues unresolved and for most that is their outlet to relax, whereas the regular Joe or Jane may relax differently. There are some people who later quit and change their life. But for now, all of your vices must be included in the budget. That's honesty and just a matter of thought. Please work on breaking those bad vices, even smoking. Take it from an ex-smoker. Remember it takes three weeks to form a lifetime habit, and it's the same timeframe coupled with a lifestyle change too that makes a big difference. However, all these things combined can make a relationship experience a time of pain during this bill crunch, coupled with getting rid of any and all vices that makes things even more emotionally charged. It's this time when one's life needs prayer, fasting, reading God's Holy Word, and praising Him until you fall out. Like when someone suggests to you to leave the public sector and go into nonprofit or private sector. That is usually the best idea to get prepared for an upgrade in your finances, and this change can bring healing in such a way that people are shocked at your countenance and more so shocked that your temperament has changed. One suggestion can change a lot and repair the damaged area called finance for some folks. For others it's other areas that healing is done from following a suggestion that pays off big, not some get-rich-quick scheme where I send you water or dirt and you send me money for a miracle that I know only God can provide and create. Around the way, we call that *poof* or *hocus-pocus*, a joke on you when nothing happens or something happens and it's not quite what you expected it to be—that's a curse.

Although there are people who use people to save their funds and avoid spending their own on the things that they want only to redirect their funds to vices. That is very dishonest. If and when one needs to obtain funds from another person, always make sure you go and pay them back, because making money means nothing when you have a stream of debts, especially after applying the plan only to not be or feel debt-free and feel like your broke, no stash and no rainy day, nor funds after that day requires one to review their financial life and prepare to be in a more comfortable position to have no debt, more funds. Plus, you do not need a friendship that depends on you because you have money. When we take our financial health seriously, we look at ourselves first, then make quick changes that will help gain financial prosperity for ourselves and the family.

When most people are in debt, do not negotiate with creditor for better payment options which benefit both debtor and creditor. Keep in mind, just ask God for forgiveness for this debt and the mismanagement of funds like in the "Lord's Prayer," which says, "Forgive us of our debts as we forgive our debtors" and to give you grace and mercy to come out of and stay out of debt. A simple prayer.

This one action incorporated with persistence in following the facts is an advice given by a lot of people. When you ask them whether it works for them, some take it and others don't. Yet there are many who do not. Only when they are left to their own devices, they actually work on everything based on their own mind-set and the stark reality which can only bring forth the greatest sound of appreciation called "It works!" I told a cousin of mine that was complaining about not having enough money, and I shared with him that poverty for immigrants in their countries of birth are poorer and American poverty is considered being rich. As long as you're born in the USA, you really don't have a valid right to say you're broke. Not even to lie! This applies to those with citizenship, work authorization, and even those who overstayed with their visas too. You're not broke, so stop repeating this lie to yourself and this doom to your finances which affects your future.

Although we don't live in their countries, we can see that they make more funds by making deliveries in our neighborhoods. It shows us that they are getting their stack on. So why can't you do the same? What's your excuse that keeps you from stacking and you don't have the language barrier either? My cousin got tired of hearing me chew him out and decided to do something. Two weeks later, he was working and delivering groceries and had a host of odd jobs that allowed for him to have a stash. It's a fact that some families do not like the rough ones that disperse the truth over their feeble excuses. My motto is, as long as you are not headed six feet below and you woke up today and every day with all your limbs working, along with all your mental faculties in check, GET PAID with dignity! I don't want to hear that you can't and that you have to borrow money to make a stash. It is a fact that you are wrong for not having a stash under the circumstances that you started a new job which requires that you have loot on hand. Yet there's a technical and tactical way which brings me to the other part that I used to share with my closest friends, family, and cool coworkers.

Being Broke Is a Sin and a Crime

When a lawyer at the firm that I worked at asked me about the job while working and asked me about taking another position, I told him that it sucks to have someone tell you after an interview that you're overqualified or the position has just been filled and a plethora of other reasons why you don't get that particular job that even your minimum qualifications should get you in the door and not turned away. However, in life, we deal with some fast balls and quite a bit of curves as well. Nevertheless, I left the lawyer with a statement that taking a job allows for you to have money in your pocket for lint to lean on. Having money prevents one from having the thirsty look like they are on a cash drought. But the most important thing to remember is that *being broke is a sin and a crime.* The council liked that as they looked at me with that examining look. Well, when asked to explain myself on the meaning of such statement, I did and discussed the fact that being broke is a sin. The book of Deuteronomy, chapter 28, states, "You are supposed to be the head and not the tail." Well, the head has all things in place or on their way to getting in place. The other fact, being broke is a crime, relates to 1905 and 1920 cases from the decision of SCOTUS where one has to have five dollars and an identification at all times. Also, it is a part of the broken windows theory from philosophy, where if a person doesn't have the bare minimum to walk around, then there is a problem. According to the standards of society, one must have funds to do anything and almost everything except stay home. Unless they have a stash, then all is well for the person to just say a prayer.

Another reason why being broke is a sin and crime because when you have to get supplies for which requires money. Since we spoke about having a stash is better and gives you leverage on a variety of levels, cash is *boss* until you run out. However, this update is for you to prepare for shortages in all areas that if this succeeds, it will be devasting, and only people who positioned themselves will be all right. Fortify thyself and take heed.

In my first book *Really?*, page 74, did speak on being prepared, and many of you have had phone calls, texts, and the sort ask: *What's next with the economy?*

Since history repeats itself, I feel that something is not too good coming forth being that February 2020 impeachment/lockdowns, and now February 2021, this is history repeating itself, and sadly, *we need to be vigilant* because this is how America was hit with the Franken Germ, and whatever it is that is coming down the pipe will affect shipping and disrupt deliveries, and if we don't pray and secure every area of shipping, America has a slight problem coming later this year going into next year that will devastate America by 2030 to 2035, and by then, it's too late for stopping this issue. The problem is going to be in shipping for everything—*prepare*. This is it… We need angels and men/women of valor in place too. Many of us need to seriously double down and get MRE foods located in the back of the book (many of you who know me asked for this, and I didn't forget you).

Stash this and integrate what you buy or get from food pantries to store-bought goods. Your house should always have bread, milk, flour, eggs, oil, rice, sugar, beans, and a Bible in your house. Being that we brace ourselves now, those who are able to eat one-shot deals using the stimulus and other requirements, set yourself into the future at least two to three years so both you and your landlord are good. They love people who pay into the future, and it's less headaches. Remember, a lease protects if you want to continue the month to month, but to pay into the future and not have a lease and be two years ahead gives you wiggle room and allows your stashes to flourish. I ask for all that read this book, please prepare cause something not too good is coming down the pipeline.

Prayer

The prayer that one needs to say is a prayer of thanks for seeing another day and being able to stick the key of your residence back into the door. With that simple prayer with faith, God makes it happen, each and every single time.

There are times in life when we feel like we are fighting an extra-long battle of financial torment, hounded, and dealing with "just barely getting by" month after month. In fact, you may not even be "getting by." You may be gradually falling farther and farther behind, and it looks impossible to catch up. But don't give up, because there is light at the end of the tunnel while stepping into being debtless.

That's why you shouldn't walk the floor at night, or take any drinks or any other thing, but there are some who will inhale some booga sugar, while others indulge to hit 420.[3] But no matter what I mentioned, prioritize changing the behaviors that lead to addiction and the things that hurt your finances and commence a change in your situation to gain ground in every action related to stashing and having the life of debt-less.

---

3 Smoke weed.

The Plan

The plan is to stop your financial fight of losing money and win the war on stashing. Where or how am I going to find the money for this? More questions arise from the fight of struggling. But today, this very plan can help you to declare war on *nothing-in-the-stash*.[4] You are not going to find it in the bank. Based on the blackout that happened in New York City in the Upper West Side, there were no forms of plastic (credit/debit cards). They weren't in full strength like cash. This is where we will correct this while digesting this book, which will guide you on financial success going forward. People may ask you, "Where did you make such great changes and strides in saving money and killing bills?" Besides saying Jesus paid it all, just say that it was an extreme antidote for healing going forward.

Project stack and stash is a tool that even the best credit repair folks don't share. Guess what, they never will share a tactic, a secret, on the nebulous tool we use daily called money!

There are several examples, jokes, and seriousness on how to see, know, and believe that God has showed up and blessed you for financial miracles (and more). Many readers like yourself need an opportunity to take advantage of some advice groomed in real tough love from those rich and others who are wealthy, whom I know personally and do not share their identities with the rest of us at all. But here's the side of action that discusses money. Understand what can happen if any country leaves the dollar hegemony. We have a serious problem over here—one that cannot be solved by Congress, military, or complaining, because our world would change and bread, food, water, and other items would soar in price through the roof like

---

[4] Marilyn Hickey Ministries. 2019. *War on Debt*. .Letter on Mark 12:41–44.

other countries in the past. Germany, post-WWII, printed so much paper money that it was totally worthless. Yes, that was in the 1940s, but ask yourself or someone, what backs our money? Hmm…don't know. Huh? Guess what? It is going to happen here, and the only thing that is wise enough to do besides preparing for the future is to watch and pray for God to lead you into what you are supposed to do for yourself, family, and those closest to you. Keep in mind that Zimbabwe, on June 26, 2019,[5] stated that they outlaw the use of the US dollar and other foreign currencies. They discussed the problems with elections, and other forms of alleged actions has prompted the government of Zimbabwe to restrict using foreign currencies for local purchases unless they change their currency. That is a serious problem and causes nations to rise up against nation, which is *part of the cause-and-effect* of Matthew 24:10. Bear in mind that other countries also do not allow other foreign currencies to be used for domestic transactions that can be settled with their country's currency. Unfortunately, we do allow deposits of foreign monies into our accounts, and several banks within New York City do accept such deposit.

[5] Zimbabwe moved from the dollar and other currencies on June 26, 2019.

Planning

When I was in the lecture hall during college and was writing my business plan, the professor thought that I was not paying attention yet realized the art of multitasking and that you can't target a person because you think that they are not mentally in the class. The professor was shocked and really wanted to see my notes on my business plan, but it was written for Jabbar Enterprises LLC now. Planning goes into money, and many times in life, we do not have detailed plan in place. Even big corporations don't have a contingency plan in place. We patronize them wholeheartedly and then orders stop. Well, like manufacturing can be disrupted, your resources can too. That's why in the chart below, we will begin a sample budget layout. Modify the chart below to meet and greet your debt into an early grave that will resurrect your finances and reduce your stress level, thus providing you and your family with more family time and less juggling numbers in your head. All this means is simply, you did not check out and you are in the house or with your family in body, mind, and soul. That's a healthy and prosperous change that really works for you and the family benefits. Guess what? It's normal to plan, pray, and enjoy your family, all the while arranging to kill your debt right in its tracks—*cold*!

Bear in mind that if you fail to plan, then you are likely planning to fail and, like we stated in my first year of college, "Failure is not an option." So as long as you pray, plan, and step into your appointed destiny, keep in mind that your stash needs to be fed. Even if you receive only welfare, food stamps, and limited cash assistance, find something or someone that needs a floor swept, mopped, and other odd jobs to do. This will help you. It is a shame that times have changed so much that you can't, like in days past, run errands for your neighbors, help a senior with their bags, and do other things that home health aides do. We need our neighbors not to be afraid and embrace each other more than how it is now. It should not come down to a pandemic or any other crisis to help those that are pillars within our communities. And for that let's continue with our new budget that honestly lists all things that you need within your cache of life and home.

Sample of Jabbar's Budget

	The Problem That Bothers the Money God Blessed Me With	Amount in Bondage before Being Freed	Minimal Payment (MP)	Divided Answer	Priority Payment	Snowball Gigantic Final Payment	Months in Bondage
1.	American Express	500	50	10 payments	None	500	10
2.	Mastercard	750	30	23 payments	None	750	23
3.	Visa	250	30	9 payments	150	300	4
4.	Phone	80	80	2	80	Same	1
5.	Rent	525	All	None	None	All	12
6.	Transportation	50	27.50	27.50	10	50	None
7.	Food	35 ([6]4 or 5)	All	None	70	100	12
8.							
9.							
10.							
11.							
12.							

[6] *Multiply by four weeks or five weeks of the month.*

Sample of Your Budget

	The Problem That Bothers the Money God Blessed You With	Pay Concessions to Bondage (Interest)	Massage the Bondage (Minimum Payment)	Divided Answer	Priority Payment Needed	Snowball Gigantic Final Payment	Months in Bondage
1.							
2.							
3.							
4.							
5.							
6.							
7.							

Using the chart on this page and below, I started the three stashes at the same time with different amounts and in different locations, plus the investment stash at the same time, all while leaving half of the paycheck in the bank. For your bills, you still have to do this although we all don't want to at times. The plan is to be able to get to one hundred singles then have small bills in these columns. The plan is to double the money that is there every week when permitted,[7] depending on how much your expenses are. Be honest with yourself because you're only cheating yourself.

---

7 It is good to have about five hundred dollars in small bills. This makes it easier to transact in case of power outages and other disasters when plastic cannot help you and cash has always proven to be boss for now. Also, if you have to borrow from yourself, always make sure you pay yourself back triple or three times the amount you borrowed. Practicing this tactic keeps you in the green via black and far away from the black. It also keeps you from borrowing and going into unnecessary debt, and others things not mentioned here. None of the tools can help unless you seriously, like my mentor stated to me. Put God first and thank him for getting you through another day, and for the night shift, seeing another day.

Jabbar's Stash

<u>Remember Now</u>: Despise not the small things…

	HALF OF THE Paycheck in the Bank for Bills	Stash 1	Stash 2	Stash 3	Emergency Stash	Money for the Future (Investments)	Starting Weeks
1.	250	7 singles	10 singles	8 singles	25	50	1
2.	250	7		8	5	50	2
3.	250	14	10	0	10	10	3
4.	250	28	20	0	0	90	4
5.	250	28	20	16	0	20	5
6.	250	14	15	24	10	30	6
7.	250	30	25	25	25	25	7
8.							
9.							
10.							
11.							
12.							
13.							
14.							
15.	SUB TOTAL	128	100	81	75	275	659
16.							
17.							
18.							
19.							
20.							
21.	SERIOUS TOTAL						

You must always have pocket money to move around with, and that may not include gas or carfare. The above chart is planned out: 1) Make you double the money every week by your own deposit into the three different stashes, (every week or two drop something on them, take out immediately all unused and unspent monies within your wallet, and put into investment stash). This helps you buy gold, silver, and can cover a credit card payment for these commodities. (2) Once you complete one hundred singles, (3) start the process all over and stash the same way, and every time you clear $100 singles, $100 in five dollar bills, and $100 in tens, and later on $100 in twenties, (4) I suggest strongly that you get a lockbox or safe (5) and make sure that it's water- and fireproof. If you bury it, *remember where you buried it! Most importantly, make sure that you have it in a safe spot.*

Sample Debt List Page

	The Problem That Bothers the Money God Blessed You With	Pay Concessions to Bondage (Interest)	Minimal Payment	Money Saved from Early Payoff	Priority Payment Needed	Done	Months in Bondage
1.							
2.							
3.							
4.							
5.							
6.							
7.							
8.							
9.							
10.							
11.							
12.							
13.							
14.							

Example Budgets

One-week employees get paid every week.

For two-week employees, every two weeks feels like your pockets are on a diet (plus more taxes come out).

Food stamps via SNAP. Too many people feel that this is a hustle, but based on food prices, I hear more people state, "I wish I can get food stamps."

Social Security disability insurance (for both retirees and disabled who get food stamps). If you live in a big city, disabled, alone, without family, friends, and great church members, then it's going to be a bit tight for you. Yet it is doable since many in NYC receive these kinds of benefits and the city is over-the-top *expensive.*

Pensions, Social Security, railroad, and other retirement vehicles of resources for their services of employment in the many areas of life, be blessed (when you're sixty-five and above, depending on the year you retire; the Social Security administration also accepts applications for those who are sixty-two and a half). This is in the facts laid out in my law textbook from college.

You can have the time and not the age, or you can have both. Just make sure that you work as much overtime for about a three- to five-year period and stack for the rainy day and the day after so that these actions taken will boast your 401K, 403K, and the long-forgotten IRA accounts too. The plan is for highly matured. And then live on a budget.

An inheritance from someone who died is bulletproof from child support in some states (the most shocking thing I learned in Family Law class, which stops vindictive parents from dragging another into court) and keeps you in control of the money. Someone I know didn't believe me until they read my Family Law textbook, which they tried miserably to keep. LMBO!

Weekly Paycheck

One thing that many budget counselors are not going to tell you is the following:

If you get paid every week, don't pay any bills yet. Pay yourself 20% of your entire paycheck. Say, you got paid $563 per week, then take out $118.60. Then proceed with the iron-clad budget that will execute more in the stash and less bills to deal with. Also, live off the entire week with 20% of your pay. In fact, don't pay your bills until your second paycheck. Unless rent or mortgage is paid, then you can execute each play in such a way that you will be like, "Wow, this really works!" It's sort of spreading the stash in a way that keeps you more comfortable and less dependent on plastic. There's nothing wrong with plastic. Just don't fall into slavery because of it. So let us begin with the reasons associated with this. You don't have a real stash that is at least six months sitting ready to pay your phone and many other bills in advance before or, as the bill is due, without using plastic or going into debt. Some of the tips that helped me gain at least six months of rent, phone, and other bills to the side were patience, discipline, and making your kitchen your first love, coupled with time. Now you understand why you should have on hand at least $100 singles and other small bills. It should be a goal to have $100 singles or dollar bills in the stash, plus money to get back and forth to work and eat, unless you bring leftovers or eat light. Why? Putting that amount of money to the side is the easy part. You seriously can stop crying and acting broke and in case, if for any reason, issues abound, you actually have cash on hand. Right now it's August 2, two weeks after the NYC weekend blackout in Manhattan and various parts of Brooklyn. You guessed it. Some who were depending on digital pay apps to plastic were not working. We all like our money to work for us, so it should work when there is a power disruption as well. That's where having funds in the stash is essential even when money seems like it's in a drought. As I finish this book, my city's social distancing order encompassed only essential workers can work and left many business owners like myself and others to figure it out. Do we play catch-one, catch-all or do we play hit-and-run which is what business owners have to face who don't sell food and have other essential services. So patiently we wait until our state opens up. But when the next paycheck comes in, then the stashing still continues to flow so that you stay on track. When you get your second paycheck, begin the process we started together. That's how I did my stashing while working for a bankruptcy law firm.

I split my second paycheck into half by leaving half in the account and taking the other half with me to stash. When you buy your carfare (or set money aside for gas[8]), you should have at least more than $250 in the stash. Not to go and buy something you don't need like most people do, but for you to have a serious stash on hand and in your bank off the grid. I applied this advice, and a few people use some of the tools spoken or combined with these same tools presented for you, which will help grow your finances of being debt-free throughout the entire book. Plus, it is uniquely designed to have a cushion and to invest with ease. Everyone wants that, but not enough people understand that having the pillow and cushion set is better than nothing. That's why it's important that if you borrow, it's to buy gold and silver. And remember that money comes to money. It is one of the main reasons that companies allow you to pay minimum amounts. The method of stashing is being so far ahead that it will shock you on having more in case of emergency. But for the day after, a stash works when plastic doesn't work. So wherever you put money at, invest and learn to keep more in your wallet or purse because it shall keep you free from slavery of debt. Phase one is discipline in your dealing with money. Make sure that you lock up your credit cards and all forms of plastic in a lockbox if you have low

---

[8] Use higher-octane gas to stay on the road longer and less in going to your pocket.

willpower in resisting spending or you lack discipline. Not following this will keep you in the slavery of debt. The methods within are not going to help you if you are not going to be dedicated to being disciplined enough to say no to items that you do not need versus the items that you may be attached to. This is not limited to smoking, drinking (social or lush), drug usage (social or out of control). All needs to get a grip on having a stash. The vices of bad habits will fall away because I commend you on trying. Take it from an ex-smoker. It can be challenging, but it all requires a change in life and socialites. All this without depending on someone to help you will make you stronger, and in fact you will accomplish winning the completion of kicking a habit and stashing furiously. Let's begin.

Operation: Feed Your Stash

Okay, for the third paycheck, you split it in half. One part stays in the bank for paying bills by phone or online, and the other part you split in half. Splitting your funds in half allows for you to stash. However, at this point you are seeing your stash *grow*. Don't spend it! Just keep it growing. Continue to feed your stash, because half of the money is going into the beginning of a joint emergency and investment stash which allows for the split of the half of what you took from your paycheck. Now dividing this into two will give you a quarter that can be applied to the emergency and investment stashes which accounts for the quarter of monies that will sit there awaiting more to come in. By the next pay week, say you get paid $563, you take out $63 and carry it with for the two days or stretch it into the weekend and review your progress if you get paid before the weekend. This is really good and keeps you from running to the bank to get more money before you get paid again. See, the objective is not to be cash-strapped. Don't always depend on plastic, and have close to a healthy $500 in the stash. This helps give you a pillow and cushion set that keeps your financial standing. It also gives you assurance if anything should happen and banks are closed. Guess what? You have funds that you have on hand, and the smaller the denominations, the better. It's easy to ask for change of ten or five than a twenty in rough times. Also, one doesn't want to seem out of place with having big bills, while others don't have the same. Don't make yourself a victim at the supermarket! Pay attention to what others are doing in glance. We shall discuss this later on. Plus, you are not taking all the merchants' change. Lastly, you don't want to seem out of place with having big bills or be like you're positioned better than others because it can be a problem for you (or them, if they act up or team up to align themselves with you like allied countries, or the contrary). You want to blend in and not be out of place. Like I tell my nieces, nephews, and first-generation cousins, always keep $200 with you as emergency or safety funds. Since 9/11, one does not need to be in a position that warrants them to talk too much, especially when you need to get to safety indoors. You can walk home from the area, hire a cabdriver, or have somebody get you out of the zone of discomfort.

After 9/11, I tell my friends and family to have funds with them wherever they may be in the nation or other nations on the earth. Always have funds because people can get you from one zone of danger to another of safety, provided you know how to travel without depending on an app or search engine. Because 9/11 happened in NYC and communications was down except for voice stream, a.k.a. T-Mobile. So it pays for one to know their city well, wherever you live and visit. Please know more than the area you live in, and if you have to evacuate, guess what, you can leave your area and go to somewhere safe and cool and return if possible.

After a newspaper article came forth during the summertime in NYC, it bothered a few of us. I must say that we all dread a day that we would have to walk out of our own area residence and move into another city, town, village, and state because of something crazy like 9/11. If it had been more destructive and required an evacuation, the influx of people into a new state would change a lot of things from economics, shelter, emergency cash assistance, and other resources. Also, nobody plans to evacuate unless it's to a new place of residence with cool people for the lifetime going forward. But back to the subject. Your goal before you pay bigger bills is to have cushion in your dwelling and security of your choice applicable to the laws of your area of residence.

Anyway, for those who get paid every week, don't take it for granted that you can't lose your job. But also know your state's unemployment laws and at least try to do three big-small things while you're working:

1. Write a goals list and complete 85% to 200% and then a new list doing the same.

2. Stack and stash a good amount of money, preferably six months of rent, mortgage, maintenance (for condos and coops). The funds need to be in an assortment of denominations that will work in times of emergency and a cut-off limit not to have low funds; like more than $200 in singles or dollar bills, $300 in fives, $300 in tens, $400 in twenties, $500 in fifties, and $500 in hundreds, and the amounts below should be your goal to meet:

    6 x $500 = $3,000
    6 x $1,200 = $7,200
    6 x $2,000 = $12,000

    Rents based on "affordable" housing (not including other necessities) or supplies. Some people who are good at saving money are people who you least expect to get their stash and stack on and be able to make investments without hoping to hit the lotto or any other sweepstakes. Being practical to work with what you have is the essence of *"Money comes to money,"* and it grows to give you interest too.
3. For every bill, small and great, that you pay off, buy a silver coin or silver bullion bars (don't ask why not gold, just look at HR 835 section 3—the last page at the bottom). Then you can buy a few karat bars at $50 to $60 dollars per piece, depending on the rate gold is going that day. Then add some gold coins in the denominations of $5, $10, $20, and $50. That requires you to purchase when the commodities market is down and the stock market is split or down too. That allows you to buy all you can afford at a lower or more relaxed price versus the higher rate when the market is up and the price is up too (sometimes depending on who you deal with as well).

The same applies to rising price to silver coins and bullion. This plan is solely for both those who just started working weekly paying jobs and people currently working; the plan works quicker when the job tips you, allowing you to feed the stash. Your entire check can be split across every lineup of stashes or, if big enough, you can live off the tips and keep a record of how much your tips are daily, because that dude named IRS does not need to be a special guest star in your life for an audit or any other reason other than paying you a refund. As a tax pro, you can keep a memo book on how much per day, week, and month are your tips and keep accurate records for your perusal. This plan can be modified to fit a heavier money flow and for you to organize your debts (rent, mortgage, gas, electric, garbage removal, water, insurance) and assets—physical money; digital money (those credit cards? Those are loans); gold; silver; land; cattle; companies that you may create, purchase, and inherit; plus anything that you invented that helps people's lives, not limited to cars, boats, or airplanes.

This type of plan clears credit cards, online shopping accounts, and other quick-to-knockout bills. The ability to get ahead, with discipline, will keep you ahead and works great too! Now prepare yourself for big windows of opportunity to come when you have $300 in the stash and $700 in assorted bills but a decent amount of $1's, $5's, and $10's works great.

It works great due to the path you traveled alone while applying discipline, patience, love, goal focus, and most of all, prayer to the equation. It all works well, and even if you don't pray, there is always time in your life to pray, just to say thank you for everything. See, there is nothing magical and no scientific formula to say thank you. For if you find it hard to say thank you, then we shall call you unthankful, and all that you work with and do shall consist of that aura. People don't like that, and it's not a good feature to have when you are trying to stack and stash some things to be a serious cushion first, then be the pillow. For the next budget, based on weekly paid, pay all your credit cards off and keep them locked in a safe. That way you are least likely to say, "Hey, I can get that and pay that off later." It takes *discipline* to accomplish this. Cook at home instead of eating out and live off credit cards. Having more credit cards in your wallets doesn't mean you're a baller or Big Willie or whatever crazy thoughts that run through your mind, especially when you can only afford the minimum. That means the interest pimps you! Remember this: there is nothing on earth that can take men, women, cities, towns, villages, states, and a country or countries into slavery BUT DEBT!

Now the next section is based on a subject which is never or hardly ever talked about.

Food Stamps via Supplemental Nutrition Assistance Program (SNAP)

Food stamps is a program that can help you get from being in a position of being between two rocks and no middle ground or leverage into a place where your back is close to being up against the wall. The SNAP program helps people, yet it is highly abused, like any good thing. The twentieth century was actually the beginning phase of the cashless society when the United States Congress during the Welfare Reform Act of 1996 signed by President Bill Clinton decided to digitize food stamps. That was to stop all the wealthy crooks from the scams of the 1980s and 1990s to figure out new methods for working the system. They also barred fast foods from taking them, and Chinese food spots also had to stop taking them. The entire program started getting tighter, until sanctuary cities and states came into existence. That changed all things and revolutionized the SNAP, allowing anyone who came from any other nation $25,000 in food stamps and $40,000 in cash, which was a package deal that came from the Social Security administration on the cash side. But the amount of food stamps during the Obama administration made this very interesting, yet I saw the changes within my neighborhood and the prejudice that ensued because of monies being doled out heavy like this for one specific culture of folks. The $65,000 came to undocumented during Obama's tenure.

Yet conversations about SNAP should not just be about how much stamps you get, "They cut dum-dum off yesterday," and other crazy conversations regarding this subject! There was a call

I received wherein a person complained that he got $200 in food stamps and then two months later they gave him $60 dollars. He wanted to sue, and I wished I really hadn't picked up the phone. That's one of those moments when I could not just give too much of my mind. Meanwhile, I was complaining that I had to write a check to the IRS for $40,000, which is someone's salary in North America. Understand the point of budgeting food stamps. The first thing you must always remember is, don't spend it all. Don't shop on the first ten days of the month. If you can wait or shop lightly, then you will see for yourself. The prices are marked up and it's not really a sale.

So whether you get $200 or $500 a month, you may truly want to apply these adjustments so you will have a surplus of $20 to $50 a month, which can allow you to stash a few items when grocery shopping and other items are on sale. The key is that the best sales is always after the tenth of the month, because unbeknownst to all SNAP recipients, all sales for the first ten days of the new month are up to a difference between a quarter to a dollar in prices. A lot of times there are majority of goods you and I use that may be bottom barrel in quality yet may help toward our goal of having more for our household and family. Bottom barrel in quality is like your toilet paper versus the store brand that's scratchy and sharp when you use it, thus requiring water to take the roughness out.

The best sales to catch are the last ten days of the month. It's like a fire sale, and you get a heavy bang for your buck. Even on SNAP, you can stash goodies for that day where shelves would be wiped clean and the stock downstairs will be depleted too! But your household is okay.

First thing first, get yourself a case consisting of six bottles of water, matches, and candles for the first month. Don't touch it! Put it in the stash. Next month, buy two more. See, now you have three cases of water in the stash. The goal is to have six cases of water in the stash and build up an adequate supply for the future. Water, coffee, sugar, tea, and other items do not have an expiration date, so secure these items while shopping for other items. Have a stash in a place where visitors cannot see it, and if you're cohabiting[9] then you need to have twelve cases of water untouched in the stash. (Same thing for children and seniors too.) Also have Gatorade and alkaline Smartwater besides the bottled water that you may stock away. There are a few people who never took my advice until they actually saw that they needed to make a few things right in their lives and have some cushion. The light bulb went off, and all they had to do was listen to my voice playing in their head. Their circumstances changed dramatically, and no one knew about growing a healthy stash while attending a two-year college. This is why it's here, before your very eyes. With a two-year degree, you can look like the bank, down low in knowing but dress muted. I will touch on this later.

---

[9] My suggestion to you living like this is to always have a crisis account, which is one of those accounts you opened while in college. You threw money into it and forgot about it. But never depend on it for survival prospects in case one has no job, gets sick and dies, or is hospitalized for a length of time. No matter what the circumstances, one must always have an account like this and a physical stash, et cetera.

Keep Your Stomach out the Pawnshop

If you have found yourself spending your entire budgeted amount to replenish the entire fridge. Days before the pandemic hit my city, I had to restock the shelves in my house. This helped to avoid the panic and clearing of the shelves like it was during hurricanes Katrina and Sandy. There is a way to change and practice discipline and patience; you will see this pay off. Don't think like there is not going to be any other money for a while. Use the SNAP benefits, spend less on that trip to the store for that week, like $40 or $50 with a ten-dollar wiggle room. Do this every week and you will see what I am talking about by next month. Trust!

When I first moved into my new place, I went to the food pantry first, then went to the supermarket to capitalize on what I obtained from the pantry. I strongly recommend to anyone who has a new place to go to a food bank and bless your house with a gift of food from the pantry. Never feel guilty for doing this one time, because this is your own "housewarming" gift to all participants of the household and the house itself. This plan worked for me when I was receiving SNAP via food stamps. It was not meant for me to live off but to get over a difficult time in my life. During a period that I was laid off and I prayed for a better day to come, those days came as the Lord provided. As a steward of the provisions, wisdom must be deployed to make everything work.

So let's think. Before you start a job and these are your last months on the state's benefit program, hypothetically speaking, this plan of action is good for you. Increase your education while you're collecting benefits and do not just collect benefits hoping that things will change. Things change when you're proactive and not just sitting, waiting for a knock on the door, saying, "Hello, this is your money, and I am here to make your pockets crowded." This will never happen at all, and if it does, good for you. But for the meantime, we must be mindful to put some work in so we can reap the benefits.

So, suppose SNAP stopped, do you have food enough to hold you and your family for a month or even two months without flipping on your caseworker or their staff? Did you expect to be cut off when you started working? If not, there's time to make things fall in place as though you were stashing for years and it was two or three months, six tops. It is totally imperative that you stop and think about your cabinets, refrigerator, and what you need to have in place before you read on further. Understand that SNAP can stop at the hit of the button or flick of the switch. When a blackout happens, and you must have a stash too. Don't just depend on this resource! Like I shared with one family member, as long as you are born here in North American soil, you don't have the right to declare being broke. Being broke is a sin and a crime! I share with many how I made money through being an entrepreneur, paper route, or helping elders with making deliveries for which they will throw you a $5 or $10 for your troubles in aiding them with their parcels. People need help and will help you when they like you, regardless if the ceiling is coming down. God laid favor on your life for this moment and to be continually *blessed.* Review, Psalm 5:12 and 37:1. Put this in your quiver.

Secondly, do you have enough canned fruit, tuna fish in oil, peanut butter, jam or jelly, bread (for the house presently), crackers for both stash and around the house in various flavors to keep your stomach out of the pawnshop? If your answer is "The blackout is for a short time," "The power will be restored soon," "Oh my, the ice cream is gonna melt," or a whole host of responses, it's time to get your mental house in order. Make a list of what you need from the store. Have a list of all the things you and your household use. Then budget $30 to $35 of SNAP with some wiggle room to spend $40 to $50 in case you overstep the pre-budgeted amount. This will allow you to build a stash and maintain your household. Of course all this means that you have to watch what, how, and where you spend the most. This keeps you with more items on hand instead of going to the store because you have the funds to do so and buy some junk snack food along with cereal. Cereal is a great food source to have and use first before going into the cabinets to cook during a storm. It works when food trucks start to get lighter on deliveries. One suggestion one mother in church always kept was to stock up on dry foods, parboiled rice (cooks in twenty-seven minutes), bags of oatmeal, grits, wheat, and other dry goods in the stash. Then she had tuna fish, spam, both turkey and ham, and other items. God bless you, Mother White. You will be missed. And thank you for providing some details to stack and stash.

Guess what, you winded up getting everything you need, spent less, have more SNAP on your balance to work with, plus the cabinets, fridge, and stash are loaded. This is what a stash does and allows for the rough times to lean on what you have in case there is an issue that will prevent electronic transfers of money like electromagnetic disruptions or blackouts. It is also good for you to have your car gassed up with premium gas so that you stay on the road longer and don't have to gas the car up. Depending on how you drive, one tank full above the F should last you for a week or two. I discussed with my brother that we should have a couple of buckets of gas just in case and we all must keep in rotation. This will allow you to be ahead while others are panicking. Some will call this hoarding, but if the shoes on the other foot. If people weren't weighed down by debt or hating, then they would be in a better position. Would they help you or maybe leave you a few items? Hmm, kindness hasn't dried up yet. Or has it?

The next thing to do is to repeat the same thing in ten days or two full weeks. When you get to the end of the month, before the next pickup, don't shop then. Watch the sale papers closely and see what I shared with you for at least two months before you shop and catch the fire sale or manager's sale too! Also, don't forget the items that are being discontinued, to make room for new merchandise. And lastly, get rid of items that are about to expire for half off as well. Always check the expiration dates on these sale items. Always rotate your food! I have seen plenty of people who do not do this; and it's wild, dangerous, and can cost you your life. Check the expiration dates on these items. Your life and your family's life depends on this action.

When the next month comes in, you will have more monies, balance, and surplus to work with. You can follow the stash guide in this section or create your own, but this guideline is to help you in case a time comes when there is a delay and everyone else is going crazy while you are just doing the opposite. It also helps to shop at spots like Costco's, BJ's, Krugger's, and other bulk item outlets which will give you more *bang* for your buck. And always use a list until you actually get good at spending a little and hauling the whole store away. Now remember, welfare is not moola to live off, and with that you need to have a super plan to get off without it being a shock and awe effect on you and your household.

Also, the SNAP has a public assistance via cash side to it. Now if you can put $25 to the stash, technically you are fulfilling scripture. This action shows and sets a future precedent that once you start working, you will carry a good habit of stashing way more than what you are putting away every pay period.

Also, it helps to further your education and, if need be, attend a GED program or attend a vocational program or a two-year college. See, when you go for a two-year degree, you get a juicy paid internship while going to school. Plus, you are collecting benefits and getting paid for learning by welfare or public assistance. The paid internship requires a budget which would allow you a gracious lump sum of funds in the stash of up to $2,000 or $2,500 per month. Just remember, if you buy all your books yourself, the more the refund of the financial aid is for you. Keep the receipts from the purchase of your books for tax purposes, and the school will issue a 1098 that you can use when you file taxes for that calendar year. Also, deduct your books and all things needed to attend school except your meals. Save the receipts for items purchased before tax season comes. After all, you do want the maximum amount afforded to you based upon the tax laws.

Now, the two-year community college degree would allow for you to stack most of the refunded financial aid monies after tuition is paid and grades are posted. All these steps help you usually after each quarter semester and the twelve-week term. The refund that is given to you after a full twelve-week semester of classes can range up to $3,500 to $6,900. Out of those amounts that need to jump into both your stash and investment stash in the amount of $750 a piece, treat yourself with $250 and use the other $250 to hang out. After all, you deserve it and you worked hard applying the heftiest plan into an action, keeping a budget that leads into a dual stash and a side stash (which backs up all the little areas needed to attack with a payment of cash or just to stash in the crisis account). All of the above depends on the state you're in and how you finesse your stashing capability that allows you to have the cushion you need. Be humble and never be broke or say that you're broke ever again.

Now for this plan to work, one has to have discipline. This is essential for those who have followed the plans for having a stash of cash and locked up their plastic (credit and charge cards) yet paid the balances so low that you can double up and have a zero balance anytime you get paid. You sleep better, your credit score is sexier, and most of all you have a hefty stash on hand. One must spend a few dollars in order for the investment to pay off and grow. See, when I was instructed to buy some gold, I didn't have a job yet or other resources to even borrow or negotiate for a time. This is where one needs a plan that will allow you to obtain a fair share of gold, silver, coins, or bullion on hand for the future. You must purchase a fair share of gold and silver on-hand in case paper money is no good. It allows you to be in a better position when there may be unforeseeable issues with the US DOLLAR and other foreign currencies. Remember, food, water, medical supplies, Gatorade, Smartwater (these items have electrolytes which your body needs, then add regular water to your body's diet later on) is going to be your personal stash to have on hand. In case something happens where one may have issues with the water and regular filtration devices, don't cut it. A stash of water and other essentials is necessary. If one thinks it is a joke, just look on my website for the list that have items that will not be on the shelves for about ninety days. That is no joke and scary too. Plus, whatever other items and security you feel is necessary for the stash, a young man on my first vacation had told me seventeen years ago about getting a gun and a few boxes of ammo. I am clueless on guns, but I do possess a baseball bat with three nails in it for house protection, and a meat cleaver too. Keep in mind that a kitchen is a *weapon of all kinds of destruction,* and that is where you really want to have things in place.

Now the main thing folks want to do is have $1,000 in the bank at all times and just to feel better knowing you can write a check and the direct deposit still keeps your account healthy. Please note that if you're getting welfare (depending on your state), you may be able to have up to $1,250 to $2,000[10] in the bank. Now, for those who want more out of life, if you go to any two-year schools, open a student account for savings, checking, and money market account. Usually as a courtesy, all fees are waived. All these mentioned accounts could be free based on the bank's offer while they are on your campus. Add the paid internship to the equation and you're saving more money than you can actually spend or give away. Now depending on your state, welfare may just keep paying the shelter allowance while you're going to school, you pay the rest of the rent, it will give you a better standing. Less stress, good grades, and safe environment are fulfillment in your life from Psalm 122:7, and a whole host of scriptures are being fulfilled by this accomplishment. That is the moment of our lives that we do not see. That's why I take time to smell any and most flowers, because most really overlook that we are all blessed to see another day. So keep in mind, every day you wake up, U ARE BLESSED!

Now if you're still being paid weekly, then you can afford to pay your portion of rent for two or three months in the future. Welfare pays the other portion monthly until you no longer meet the pro-

[10] Some of the other states may have lesser or more specifics on monies to keep in the bank. Make the best of the time in school while being out of debt, because the next moves you make in life will be over-the-top and your life will be aligned with the scriptural command for mankind to be fruitful and multiple and subdue the Earth (see Genesis 1:26).

gram criteria and have a comfortable salary like $50,000 or $60,000 per year, plus a degree. Then make sure you contact your case worker to let them know you have a real job with a salary and thank them for the help. Don't forget to be thankful for the help. Ask if you can keep the medical coverage for the rest of the year. If the say yes, good, and if they say no, then so be it. At least, you have a job that pays bread.

Now get ready to embrace your new life, because the steps of a righteous man, woman, or child are ordered by the Lord. This has been my understanding in making things happen. God has been great in allowing all of us to see another day, healthy, happy, and ready to get our plans started to secure a great future. That is always the plan. The other part of the plan is to always be able to put your keys in the door of your residence.

Hopefully, you are close to graduation, coming off welfare, with a job and a healthy stash of gold, silver, cash in a variety of denominations, and about $1,500 in the bank.

Now it's time to plan out what new goals you want to accomplish. If you're behind in rent and live in a place like New York, the HRA or DSS may be able to help you with a one-shot deal to pay for back rent. Remember, you do have to pay that money that was loaned to you for back rent, which will keep you in good standing with the government agency. Now in some states, there are people who have obtained a four-year degree while collecting benefits. But just to be on the safe side, look at your agency's public assistance rules and regulations about obtaining a degree or two. Caseworkers like it when a client is motivated to make it happen, and some will guide you to success. Even if you get teased about having an associate's degree, no one knows that you're working on your debt-free financial portfolio and can always go to a four-year school *debt-free* and *without getting pimped* into taking an educational loan. If you want to attend a four-year school, do it with a scholarship and pray that all secret things that are not discussed therein is revealed for you to achieve success and prosper as thy soul prospers.

Higher Pay Plan for Weekly Paycheck of Stashing

To either invest or just till it grows fur.

I worked for a law firm, let's just say to take care of the dirty laundry of the attorneys and accountants as well. While working there I looked at a few factors: rate of pay, days off without pay, paid holidays, vacation, paid sick leave (based on new legislation from NYC Council and NYS lawmakers, plus other legislation that may alarm you), working hours, office environment, travel time (to and from the office), and time to unwind (shopping, eating, dating, et cetera), after-work treats and moments of love to do both by yourself and with that special someone. Make sure you have great places where the food, service, and all stay on point, and next to perfect so you can get paid with a smile upon the contract being signed. Your client always remember you every time they eat where the deal was finalized. But I will leave that for further discussion later.

Most of all—knowing how much your credit card bills is very essential to keep track of those items of plastic in the safe or lockbox and now your adding on to your stash, monies that you have accumulated previously. Depending on hourly rate, perks, bonuses, and other cool things companies give them an incentive that shows the company cares about its employees. Knowing all this can work out well for you as long as you stick to the plan of stashing.

Now if there are other things that are missing here, it's fine because this is a suggested overview rough draft of the upgrade in your life both financially and publicly.

When I got paid on Thursday, that paycheck was used to purchase more time on my metro card for the NYC MTA so I can go to work without hassles or asking friends (asking is cool when you have the intention to pay back or give an equivalent to the funds borrowed).[11] Keep two credit cards with you for your first two weeks before removing them from your wallet and only keep your debit card. (If you're on public assistance and working within the realms of the laws to collect that resource, attend school, and work a paid internship, all works for you.) Yeah, I know I told you to put all those credit cards in the safe or lockbox; however, many of us keep a credit card with low interest rates, no fees, and with a lower limit card. It's good for you to get gas and light things, but the purpose here is to get you from plastic that costs you fees, interest, and loss equity. This is something that needs to be reinstated back to you, which adds value to you. If you have credit cards, each time you pay them off increases your credit score. The higher your score, the better banks look at you as low risk. Plus, all and any loans that you take have low interest or no interest charged either, which is the best outcome!

Also, banks have been known to give low interest fee, and they have assisted great number of clients. But as I spoke to my good pals and mentors, it's not a major loss, which is good. A few women and men have done the same tactic so they don't go over the limit and the card automatically rejects the transaction when they're close to the maximum limit. Depending on how long you have had the account, they may give you some wiggle room.[12] Just make sure that you are able to get back to your state/town. If traveling outside your regional area and you place a call to the creditor to help extend your limit until you are able to get home, they will do it for you. It only takes a call to the card issuer, and they will give you a green light so you can get home. It happened to me when I went over the limit and

[11] I will explain the significance of this later. There is a purpose why you have silver and gold and allies that help aid you to financial stability. Remember, millionaires help millionaires.

[12] Some credit card companies will extend your limit when it's an emergency, especially when you are out of town and your purchases are coming from a different state. Keep in mind: always build rapport with the banks that help in times like these. It works too, depending on the length of time of the account. Keep that in mind before traveling.

they allowed me to get the gas so I can get home with the family at that time.

Okay, now the lesson.

When you're paid, look at how much you're paid after taxes and other deductions. Say for example you get paid $1,000 after taxes, deduct 20% of your pay to pay yourself 20%. That will be equal to $200. Then look at what's left: $800. Now take $300 off that and apply it to all your triple stash for your investment and emergency stashes simultaneously and use the 20% to tide you over until next payday. That's why it is important to keep a separate note pad or use the pages within this book where you can jot down all thoughts that will help you succeed. List or record the amount of bills paid, and once paid, don't make any new bills. Just put monies to the side because we are going to return and discuss the reason of having the pad recording bills entirely paid.

Deducting your 20% for yourself and $300 for your triple stash leaves you with $500. Now take from the bank $100 in singles as you get closer toward your next payday and stash it. This will leave you with $400 ready to cover rent, mortgage, taxes, and other reoccurring bills. With the absence of stress or worry, applying discipline goes a looonng way. Remember, if you want a stash, one must sacrifice reckless spending and be honest with themselves. It will help you a hundred percent, and you will be happier, not stressed.

For next week and next payday, you repeat the same thing, but now you decide to continue carrying your two credit cards and your debit card with you, which is good. But discipline is the hidden rule that keeps more cash with you instead of away from you. Now I am going to walk you off depending on the credit as an emergency instead of having cash on hand plus other components that attract money to you for your stash, investing, and being debt-free. Remember, money comes to money!

You are paid for working, it's next week's payday, you have money, small bills are paid, and your fridge is not crying for replenishment. Now that you have a stash of $100 singles, money to go to work (carfare), and you have made payments on your plastic you carry and the ones you don't, you should begin to lighten your wallet or purse by leaving all the extra plastic locked up or call it social distancing from your slave masters. Yep, you read it right; those very credit cards are your slave masters when you *borrow* from them and you are subject to paying them. So this act of *financial social distancing* is your only key to survival going forward and allows for you to prosper with more liquid which is cash, clout, bread, dough, or the bag. No matter what you call money, it is the blood of keeping your shelter, food, and security from the diablos of the world. So by the next payment, you're stepping highly over the minimum which allows your interest rate for borrowing money from plastic to be reduced big time. Once your balance is lower than $150, always pay yourself every time that you get paid with 20% of your entire pay and work with that. Leave the rest of your pay either in the bank or bring some of it to the stash. It's a choice that you have to make, and like my elders stated, "You want to keep your money close to you.[13]" Plus, you are more relaxed physically, mentally, and economically too. You will be smiling more because your recession- and depression-proof plan works for your present finances. And you have both a stash for emergency and investment simultaneously while living your life blessed.

When this next week begins, you can expect to take 20% funds for your personal pay. Now take all unspent or non-allocated monies out of your pockets, wallet, or purse, and begin to stash that money you took out for a safe place to keep at. If you have $20 leftover from last week, take that and start stashing for your investment and emergency, which will grow seriously bigger than previously. Keep repeating removing unused monies from your wallet before payday and place it in the investment and emergency stashes. For example, you have $125 and need to break it down into a spread of twenties, tens, fives, for your new stash. This stash is different from $100 singles in the stash. It's the *investment stash* where some or a portion is

---

[13] My elders had a talk about investing into foreign markets, and they were against it. Personally, just do your homework before you spend a dime. If it looks too good to be true, then it's a problem with the glass sandals and you need to have your size and what works for you. There is no simple formula to getting rich other than "put that work in!"

divided into the *emergency stash.* Review the chart on stashing. This split would be $62.50 going into both at the same time because you are preparing to build more than two stashes and have a nest egg for each month you're working, which is good. Throw another $100 singles into the stash with that lonely single stash. Now your stash is looking prettier, and you don't have the thirsty I-need-money look! Just remember that notepad of bills paid entirely helps. It will reflect the facts of progress made, and that is not for you to just slack on applying the pressure on your finances because the total number is going to be bigger than what you started out with. In time, you can take all the amounts, add them up, and make a solid goal to obtain the same in your stash and at least half in both checking and savings, just to show creditors and banks that you have something swimming in the accounts in this digital age. If in the future, the nation decides to digitize our currency, then it would be best to have some gold and silver in your stash. Like I told my cousin when he asked me what to buy with his new credit card, buy silver coins and some gold coins, then pay the bank off and laugh. You have accomplished wealth on a level different from what the hood spoke on, and it's quite pretty. It was created when the earth was, so it belongs to God first. Just keep in mind that when you eat a meal, you take one bite at a time. Well, this is a financial tactical stack and stash for two areas of your life: emergencies and investing. Many people don't have stashes labelled such yet, but you will be the second after me and it starts with some things small growing into more than before. I remember this while writing the same book you're reading which allowed me to double up stacking. I positioned myself and others into being wealthier than the present, and in the future be without stress, worry, asking for funds or depending on someone to give me money all the time, and more.

Next, you're going to do like the rich and prepare yourself for a phase out of paper. That is anything metal which holds a better staying power financially when times are rough. Look at that pad you have been writing down which bills are completely paid off. Well, say you killed three bills entirely, it's time to replace that money with a substance that will attract more money to you.

Money Comes to Money

I took the amount of a bill, fully paid it, which was $200, and went to govmint.com to buy four-karat bars.[14] This purchase allowed me to have a small amount of gold bullion because I did not "despise small beginnings." When I received the gold, it went into stash. That same day I received $200 in the mail unexpectedly and $200 in tips, because I was working at this time as a delivery guy for a grocery store. Now these unexpected monies will not happen to you unless you're seriously tired of having no funds. Where-my-train-is-coming-in thoughts will leave because it's placed in your heart by the good Lord, and you can't shake it until you do your job. Then it will happen. When I did this plan in the early years of the Obama administration, I was climbing out of debt, staying out, and helping others to learn the discipline to stack, stash for emergency, investment, and (super) stash. The plan worked well. In my first book I discussed a plan on how you can live off your tips, stock funds for emergency, stash, and when that infamous rainy day all comes together you are different and looking for the days after the rainy day. Applying this plan will literally allow you to be sitting while receiving and growing economically, and you are phasing out a percentage of paper to being in a better position going forward. See for example, you sit down and reevaluate the entire count of your new stash, which is more attractive now because you have added gold coins or bullion, some silver, $400 singles, $350 (twenties, tens, fives), and a separate $250 in

[14] Later on, with the same company, I purchased ten silver eagle dollar coins and that made my stash in metal stand at $400 in cash paid but its value was about $750, which is cool and allows money to come to money continuously! It is about being humble and not wearing the money. Yeah, that is a serious subject, and yes, it will be discussed but not now.

fifties and hundreds. That equals to *one thousand dollars*! That's more than what you didn't have before. Plus, a loose amount of money that will add into the $350 dollars gets retired for not being used. By the time your next paycheck comes to you, just repeat the same pattern until it becomes natural to pay yourself 20%. Also, you have been putting your funds into an engine powerhouse of *not ever being broke*. That means less stress for you and a better position going forward despite whatever happens in the markets and economic models of Nasdaq, S&P, and the Dow on the American markets versus the foreign markets. You have a stash of funds that is there when two or four months ago, you didn't. Repeat the process and modify it as you see fit.

This abovementioned plan can also be capped with an IRA of $500 to $1,000. You can use your credit card and take a cash advance to purchase an IRA (where you can specifically double down on repaying the monies and you wind up having a good credit score, great payment history, an IRA account, and an active credit card account, increased credit based on how long you want to keep paying the cash advance back. Once it's paid back, then you have an IRA paid for by a credit card cash advance instead of chancing it on stock and waiting for a return to make a payment on your credit card). This is a plan that keeps you in your financial lane to stash and keeps you moving forward and never saying that you're broke! At this moment you have some financial strength but not quite where you want to be at. These plans are serious enough that worked for all of us to stash in the beginning and continue to work for family and friends that having a budget and loot in the stash allows for less stress, which is *great*. For without a stash, one would have the thirsty I-don't-have-or-get-money-quite-like-you look. By actions alone, you are showing that you don't have a budget or credit or can borrow $10,000 without a question from the person that loaned it to you. This plan gives you a *chance* to have liquid on standby. Basically it is on you to make it happen. If not, then you are assassinating yourself and your household from financial freedom. Also, somewhere close to six to nine months of keeping plastic in good standing allows the issuer to increase your limit, and that means the bank trusts you enough to loan you more of their money. This doesn't mean that you have free money to go on a shopping spree. There have been too many people in life who do this instead of using their loans to create wealth for the future. Credit cards are a tool that can help you when used to obtain financial leverage. I did it, and it works only if you apply discipline each and every day.

Now for those who are saved and who have made Jesus Christ as their Lord and Savior, you are mandated from biblical constructs and provisions to tithe. "Render unto Caesar his" is the model (applying biblical principles). Whether you started working a new job or returned to your old one after the Franken Germ and you found out that you get paid every week, the pieces are always going to fall into place now. Look at the same list of cares and concerns (keeping the armour of God on, blessed oil, and a great reference Bible with a concordance is necessary). Remember for this next plan and process, I get paid $1,000 after taxes. Now you follow how all the pieces come together and see if you can establish the same flow. You can write a goals list, a game plan that works well for you, and more in this book.

The Running Plan

The pay is $1,000 and after taxes and other deductions you come back with $563. The first paycheck is used for obtaining carfare for back to work, some lunch money to relieve the stress of using your credit card, and not as much stress going into next week. I didn't pay any bills (rent and mortgage is necessary to pay). After all my bills are low and are paid ahead of time, well, it's time to take $250 and split it into two stashes. The last two are going into one more. That one is stashing singles. Trust me, it works out in weird and hard times. Now on next week's payday after you worked the whole week only to keep your stashing plan active, out of a pay of 563 after taxes were deducted, take out of the bank $63 to carry you through the affairs of that day. If you're going out, you need to mindfully consider that this is your second check and to deviate from your course of stashing will prolong being in a highly better position that allows you the financial flexibility to dictate what and where you may want to spend or just review everything pertaining to your financial affairs. When your money is sound, you make more sound decisions instead of saying, "I had it, but where did it go?" and "I am going to do this," only to not do it. Your attitude changes because this allows more solid decisions than ones born of sacrifice, which brings provisions to have on hand. Remember, money is a nebulous tool, which means it has no emotional attachment. Some use it as a weapon, whereas others use it wrongly; but for now it is the blood that keeps the roof over your head and the roadmap that keeps your pockets full like a file cabinet of files! That's the objective you must keep in mind in its entirety to ensure you that you can never state to anyone that you are broke, not even to yourself, especially when you don't have funds at that moment. It's a bad habit that in many neighborhoods in different cities and states, people have funds and cry broke and they lie to themselves, activating an evil to attach and become a stronghold in their life. See, we give power to words that we speak; it works for evil and for good. It is better to state that you are on low funds with those that you love and care for than to state that you're broke. You give power into the words of death to your finances when you say you're broke when you're not instead of saying you're just low on funds.

In plenty of households, too many people always speak the wrong crazy things into their lives and wonder how. The other thing is to remember that money circulates and you have to make sure that when you circulate it, to resolving a bill, it is coming back to you in many forms and even when you least expect it. That's why tithers always tithe, because with the 10% they tithe, the 90% is blessed and comes back with interest that impacts their household, family, and more. Double interest comes back. See Malachi 3:16 and Leviticus 27:30 (interest if you borrowed the tithes for business purposes). God is a businessman. Stop hating because many new businesses have borrowed tithes and prospered. My favorite is, "Give, and it shall be given unto you, good measure, pressed down, and shaken together, and running over, shall men give into your bosom" (Luke 6:38). This is the legal financial premise for reaping interest each time you give. Don't limit yourself to just a tax write-off either! Go and get your blessings and have a great day!

Now, back to dividing the $563 by withdrawing $63 for that payday and half the funds from the account that will be split into two. But the real split comes by dividing $250 by two and taking that $125 for the investment and the other $125 for emergency stashes consistently for ten weeks straight. You will have more in your financial arsenal so your second stashes should have $500, $1,000, or more, with a foundation of $200 in singles. If you followed the previous lesson, buy some gold and silver. Trust the facts that having things in place beats not having them. For this and other examples just recall the long lines when hurricanes Katrina and Sandy were on the way. Your sacrifice made now helps your household advance in so many ways that many people don't know about. But the Federal and state agencies have advised many residents of NYC to get and keep an emergency food, water, and other provisions in the stash. Right now, China is telling their people to stock up on food for three to six months, and our president for three years has been telling people to stock up since being in office. Regardless of folks thinking you're a prepper, they are mad and will consider coming at you wrong when times are rough. This is serious advice that friends change and so do others when they are desperate. But by taking these few steps you know that you and your house shall be saved because you adhere to sound advice and not hate or panic. Well, sound advice keeps you in the having and not in the lacking that primarily keeps you from being in a panic like the rest of the people around you. It's okay to be nervous, but to panic is a problem. That's why stacking up to more than $1,250 can be your first stash and, say all your bills are paid off, the only bills you have is rent, phone, food, life insurance. Whatever you or others may have that comes under control for discipline and consistency is the key to achieving having and not being in lack. If you have any vices, smoking, drinking, eating excessively, and others, read 2 Timothy 14–15 (AMPC), "Alexander the coppersmith did me great wrongs. The Lord will pay him back for his actions. Beware of him yourself, for he opposed and resisted our message very strongly and exceedingly." Paul was being told that Alexander the coppersmith had did him some wrongs. Well, applying these scriptures on all the vices that came up against your finances, beware, for these will oppose and hurt your finances. These vices can cause contrary and bad results. Resist vices or bad habits, especially when you want a better future.

Remember, as long as you work, you must always feed your stash, not just your 401, 403k, IRA's, and even when or if you should be unemployed! This is for you to live, invest with ease, and not be broke or depend on credit cards or loans unless you have a strategy to pay it all back before the banks' prorated map to their interest clock begins.

Once you do all the things necessary to have a couple of grand in the stash and you're on the second and third stashes to load up, this very plan can allow you to invest into precious metals or the market which will diversify your portfolio in life, and you will hardly ever be stressed about not having money in the stash. See, one thing about having precious metal or stock in the stash is it makes paper money come quickly without any delay. It is setting an alignment of having it come out of circulation into your hands with interest. In the Bible, Mark 4 talks of the three servants and what they did with talents. A talent at that time is another form of money, yet the parable shows you the outcome for the servant who doubled money based on the last one who just hid it. Sounds like many of us go through the same thing—put money in the bank, only to not get interest and be charged a fee for holding your loot or take money out of the bank to avoid a lien on funds. My Family Law class favorite is the removal of funds from a divorce. Most divorces end due to money and later infidelity and because the relationship went bankrupted! One can still bounce back in time. Yet many people do not pick out the one who will be by your side when it comes to discussing money. Sadly, many people find out too late that they have some things that can be financial time bombs which need to be defused before they get out of control. The two never took stock until the plague of Franken Germ kicked in and showed people who they really have by their side and others learned some things too. That sucks to a level beyond understanding when you learn that the one you are in love with is dead investment, especially masking it while dating.

One important thing I do before it goes in the stash is to pray over it, then make great strides to use it as the tool that it was intended to be, without ever saying or being broke. It's a talent to know how to flip money and make a profit, but it is not hard to do. The example in Mark 4 directs us to look at the Bible, in Psalm 34:10, for encouragement: "But those who seek the Lord shall not lack any good thing." This will always carry you going forward in life and that's why it's important to pray. The writer of Psalm wants us to know the facts that seeking the Lord will bring good results than when we do things on our own. Always pray that God keeps his angels to guide you and watch the results going forward.

Look, I took the time to take my entire paychecks for three weeks and pay my rent by writing out the check for the more than three months' rent. This was setting the groundwork for paying rent for more than three months into the future. That way, all summer, I don't have to pay rent and I can do whatever I want. That's not just a declaration; it's a reality that works following this plan. That way all the money that you make going forward is split between food, water, items for hygiene, stash, donations to nonprofits, phone bills, dating, children, visiting people, and travelling anywhere comfortable within the country. And if you have T-Mobile, then you can get T-Mobile Tuesdays that allows beyond great deals and deep dish discounts!

Another thing to remember is that at some time, you can take a list of all the bills you paid and contact the precious metal companies that are within this book for silver/gold eagles or bullion to purchase and throw in the stash. Start small. When you throw these items in the stash, remember they are there for two reasons.

One is to have more wealth in your stash. Despite what happens in the market, you are good. Also, depending on where you live, it can buy you food, gas, and a whole host of things. You can't help everyone, but you can advise them going forward to stash!

Second is when the paper money is no good and the only real source of finances that keep you and your family eating is gold and silver. Check out HR 4827 on the topic of cash and see the true reason why gold would take a hard hit is because of HR 835 section (3) where gold is attached to back up our money. I submit these laws to you because you're not going to get this information on the news, social media, and alternative news. When paper money is no longer good, then one can do these things that others will be desperate, and you can join them only to allow them to see you in public. This one act keeps you from being a victim unnecessarily, and in the land of vigilance gold can be used to pay taxes for the big items like houses and land and silver for everyday items. That way you own the item and you don't have to barter, at least not yet or ever, depending on how you position yourself. Countries have been looking at cryptocurrencies. I am personally against it because as long as we have nukes, electronic money and computers would be in bad shape. (EMD is less disturbing while EMP is more disturbing and will set a society back into the stone ages.) I share this with you because if we are going to be a cashless society, you want to be in good standing going forward. However, I do implore you not to take the chip[15] in your right hand or forehead, or else you're doomed! The Bible does speak about this. They will advertise it innocently, and some companies are trying to get their employees to get "chipped." Many have sued and won, and they have a card to waive in front of doors, elevators, and other places that unlock. Besides that, the only chip that's going in my body is a tater chip, right in my mouth! Praise God! Give him praise and glory!

To understand the agenda of chipping, read pages 1510 to 1513 and page 2000 of HR 3990, which discuss and expand on it in brevity. Make no doubt about it. NYC Transit has it and so do other places like supermarkets. They have it for time clocks in office buildings. Public and private sector alike are using a biometric system called inventory accounting interlinked with artificial intelligence (AI). The full rollout of this program was halted by many people who voted for President Trump, who voted for a better economy than two hundred in food stamps and weird laws which stunt economic growth and hurt our land. Funding all types of atrocities all needed to stop so people can come out of debt and live instead of struggling. Also, our president eliminating the mandate for Obamacare changes the amount of hours one has to work. Instead of twenty or twenty-seven hours a week, you can get thirty-five or more than forty hours. The economy has worked well for many of us before the plague came through from the other side of the world, and the American socialism trial shall soon be over once we go back to our new livelihoods.

Remember, be fruitful and multiply and subdue. They are key components of being productive that brings resources and that can double or triple ownership. See, what and how that phrase "fruitful and multiply and subdue" is not equated to socialism or communism, so both isms are not and would not help you to get your stash on. Besides, you are supposed to prosper and be in good health.

---

[15] See ID 2020 Alliance. Taking a vaccine comes with a microchip, so when you can't have one without the other. It will be entering into a contract with your own freewill on the promise of healing, safety, and security of your bio data from being hacked. Daniel Laurino, thank you.

Anything contrary to doing better is contrary to you and the rest of humanity, point-blank.

Too many of my friends and classmates who were being evicted were happy that Trump became president, and their lives improved twentyfold more than all eight years of Obama. This was the perfect time to work out all the things that was on hold and fix the kinks and give you a word from the wealthy and rich that is to stack money. Stack money. We all must bear in mind that our bills need to be paid ahead to stay in the black and not the red. But how many people live the vicious cycle of getting in debt only to wallow in it is beyond me. The most important thing that we all must do is not only to prepare our hearts and our minds. However, the Bible shows us to prepare. Joseph did it in Egypt when they went through the seven years of good before the seven years of famine. So having money, gold, silver coins or bullion in the stash is the coolest thing, and it prepares wealth to come to your family replacing struggling like you did before. Plus, having food, water, coffee, tea, and other items that won't expire for years in place is, like I shared with my elders, better to have it and not need it than to need it and not have it. People don't have to know everything that is going on with you. That's why there is a ninth constitutional amendment that discusses privacy. This is something that doesn't need social media's eyes, but it requires us to be better stewards of what we have and cuts the filibuster crap out of our presence.

Bimonthly Payday of Stashing Without Stress

Okay, so you thought I forgot about the every-two-week employee? Nope, in fact the same plan that works for those who get weekly pay works for you too. Understand that most upper-paying jobs, careers, and even some internships pay their staff every two weeks. Even works better when you throw tips and other perks that expand and help your loot climb up into your stash too. It all counts!

The following is very cool, and because God has showed me how this works, you are going to love it. That was during the time I was working for a union job. Since the SCOTUS decision, the union couldn't take out union dues. The union was democratic and I am conservative and they knew this for a fact. Plus their HRA knew that because of this court decision was a fastball into a grievance and then a lawsuit if unresolved or retaliation is done to cause you to lose your employment. That is a serious EEOC matter, where the number one in New York City is a cool attorney named Jeffrey Goldman. He is top in his field, and Epstein Beckerhoff & Green is the fourth in this field as well. These names are on top of the field of discrimination law. They know their ways beyond EEOC matters for the NYC and also within the nation. Now, working at a valet allowed me to get my stack and stash on! But it took time and patience and staying within my means. Exercising discipline and strongly resisting all types of temptation of shopping for more than basic necessities is just the beginning of having more, and it's good to have more than being in the land of lack. Once positioned properly and financially, coupled with killing all the bills that was created by yourself (or your family), pay all insurance and phone bills way ahead to give your pocket a moment of relaxation that will be help for those moments. That means, in the entire course of a year, can you actually put one or two full paychecks to the stash? If not, then it's time to make some better adjustments and apply the 20% rule every time you get paid. Please remember to stay within your means and that the only way you have a stash is when you put something into it.

And you will like having the moments to teach your friends who will want the advice from you instead of figuring out how to borrow money from you, which some of them either can't pay back or have no intention of paying back. It sounds sad and it's bad, but it happens in life.

The sample list below has a few items that we all pay for in our various lifestyles such as rent, mortgage, gas, electric, and other items listed below. It's always better to pay life insurance three months to a year which frees up funds for other things in life and keeps you from digging in your pockets and allows you to be in a better position in life. This also gives you less stress and enables you to pursue fulfilling things in life that are conducive to growing. Once you have this mind-set and focus to keep your finances in check, it will benefit you greatly. The other most overlooked factor is that you must teach others who have issues with finances the same methods, since we know that most people are not going to blatantly talk about money or the lack thereof. It is strongly advised that you guide them to being financial fit as a true friend. The other conversations are for parents with children when it comes down to the world of finance.

Sample Debt List Page

	The problem you got into (DEBT) NAME	Full Payment	Minimal Payment	Quarterly Payments	DOOMSDAY Payment	Money Saved in Change Jar	Months b 4 I'm FREE
1.	Mortgage or rent						
2.	Gas						
3.	Electric						
4.	Food / Snacks						
5.	Carfare to work						
6.	Life /car/ home-rent/ INS[16]						
7.	Stash						
8.	Stash / Investment Funds						
9.	Hobbies						
10.	Entertainment						
11.	Dry Cleaning						
12.	Leftover Unspent Monies						

The above list is the start to have an idea before you interview for a new job or go back to work. When you hear numbers, then you can give a bona fide answer which will get the ball rolling for you to start unless you have another interview. Then send a thank-you letter after the interview and give an answer after you have concluded all your interviews for the best-paying spot that will give your bud-

16 Insurance for life, auto, home, and all insurance does not cover EMP's and acts of terrorism either.

get listed above an idea of how much you're going to be stashing as well as what you are making. This can help you use your tax refund for vacation or investing. It will show what you made that year, like your W2. What you have in the stash is what you shored away. That includes the bank accounts too. It all is relevant for your stash. Now basically tackling any bill that can be paid ahead will help you because you're going to actually save money to a point where your first bundle of funds saved should be like $1,500 to $2,500 within a six-month period. You will be making about $4,000 to $4,700 per month before taxes. After taxes and health insurance are deducted, you're left with about $1,200, roughly speaking, before the next payday within two weeks.

The goal is the parallel, how do I build a stash on top of what I have or what I don't possess at this current moment yet? What will I have shortly? Do I have all the tools to meet and exceed the goals mapped out? These are questions that I shared with a family member who was shocked at the lineup, but it was a wake-up call that allowed him to get his finances in order and growing! In the beginning it may seem a bit rocky, with money being loose enough to cure tight problem areas of life. Positioning is essential and keeps you from living paycheck-to-paycheck into living off one paycheck and skip a month or two. From one-month pay, then you don't touch your pay for three months. Unrealistic? Not really. With discipline, you can do like many Africans have shared with me. They pay one-year rent in advance. That is sweet! That's how you keep from living from paycheck-to-paycheck. Another thing is worthy of thought. If ever one is going to be unemployed, then it should be more than enough to cover your rent and other low bills. Stay within your means and you can stash over half of what you get paid. Well, say you get paid $4,000 a month but after taxes you see $2,500 and change a month. That's $1,250 and change every two weeks. So how do we start a stash? Even from a temporary job—valet attendee or delivery clerk—you can have a stash too. List all the bills you have plus travel expenses, groceries, and money for popup deals before the pay period. It is all a blessing.

Say you start your stash with $100 in singles first (don't touch it, or you pay back three times for the penalty of borrowing), then in the course of stashing, you may want to make a list and keep track of the stash you are building for investments across the board. When you made the declaration to get your stash on, it's on!

I started my stash from whatever I had in my pocket, wallet, and some loose change lying around on a table somewhere in the house. Yes, that lost 3.65 cents is a starting point for your three stashes growing at the same time with goals ranging from $100, $500, and $1,000 all while your armed with your job that feeds your bills. Make a list to powerhouse through, review it, and the goal to stash or exceed. Keep in mind, I followed this plan while working a job that lasted two and a half months and was able to accomplish the list of the numbers shown above. Before the company was sold, I was able to have $400 in pocket money, which I did have to dip into the stash. I was able to replace that dip with triple. Borrowing 100 and returning 300 back keeps one from borrowing and makes the stash fluffy, but most of all, it's the triple penalty imposed by you for dipping into the stash. You do pay the pimps at the bank for borrowing their money. Well, pimp your pocket, remembering paying yourself *three times* for the amount borrowed. This chart is called the reoccurring weekly and monthly:

Reoccurring Weekly or Monthly

	The Problem You Got Into (Debt's Name)	Payoff Amount	More Than Minimum	Quarterly Payments	Doom's Day Payment	Money Saved in Change Jar	Months in Bondage
1.	Mortgage or Rent						
2.	Gas						
3.	Electricity						
4.	Food/Snacks						
5.	Carfare to Work						
6.	Life/Car/ Home/Rent Insurance[17]						
7.	Stash						
8.	Stash/ Investment Funds						
9.	Hobbies						
10.	Entertainment						
11.	Dry Cleaning						
12.	Leftover/ Unspent Monies						

The stash needs the beginning foundation of $100 singles in place, and then everything can go well and better. The first $100 in stash could keep your mouth from saying that you're broke. Just look at all the buildings around you; they all have a solid foundation. That's what you want, so let's start this new agenda of stashing set forth with the following amounts:

100 250 500

[17] Insurance for anything that has a policy and deductible attached to it.

Are the new goals for your three stashes to begin the same way or different? How much can I put in each or spread out? And can I feed these three stashes monies left from the previous payday to go into a fourth/fifth stash called investment and emergency stashes? It's as essential as opening a checking or an IRA account. The only thing that makes the numbers work is discipline, patience, time, prayer, and predetermined mind-set to accomplish your goals, without getting sidetracked into things that are dead investments.

If you're not serious or focused on stashing money, all the energy devoted to reading this book was not a waste. It is an investment that only you can benefit. Others benefit when you share the knowledge, but bear in mind that times when you get paid and put nothing to the side is a waste beyond energy and time. It's a waste of your stunting your financial growth, and that is where the truth comes out when payday after payday contrary to stashing is leading you into financial death.

Ask yourself this questions:

> Do I have anything in a stash? Can I make it without a stash or living off the land (using people to do things for you instead of getting things in gear for yourself, profits you nothing in return)?
>
> Why do I need a stash? I make a lot of money per month after rent/mortgage is paid.
>
> Do I have investment money without using a credit card?
>
> Do I have any silver or gold to cash in for cash in case times get tough and rough?
>
> Is there money enough in my 401k, 403k, IRA accounts, or did the market take a downturn and leave me with nothing?
>
> Can I get to work with no money, and for how long?

These are serious money and future questions that every man, woman, and child (many are on their own), and many cultures do consider going forward. What will happen when everyone is out of a job is wild and makes me think back to the Great Depression of 1929, but I can't wrap my brains around it because I wasn't born during that time. But if that time was rough, this plan will keep you straight to not be in dire straits.

Once-a-Month Budget

The budget for once a month is as follows:

Rent	$1,400
Tithes/Offerings (Donations to Nonprofit Organization)	$400
G & E	$100
Carfare	$50
Phone	$100
Food	$200
Laundry/Cleaners	$50–$100
Medical Deductible	$250
Hygiene Products	$75
Entertainment	$100

Stashing $250 to $500 a month

This budget represents a pension of roughly $7,500 a month without Social Security. There are people who receive this type of income but seriously need to review their budget and frequently too. Use the charts in the later part of the book and notes to keep you on track while you win at accomplishing your goals.

The abovementioned budget is written with the component of tithes and offerings, which is based on Malachi 3:10 for tithers and Galatians 6:6 where an offering can be any amount for those who are not too familiar with tithes. Lastly, the Word tells us in Matthew 6:38 that when you give, it comes back to you (the law of circulation with interest). For both Christians and non-Christians will be blessed, tax write-offs, et cetera. Amen.

Prosperity

Sometimes in life, we exhaust all types of avenues to obtain and maintain the items we have and want to achieve, yet there are times resources run low, requiring help from other sources without using a person or disrespecting one's self. There are some people who are in dire straits; they turn around only to concoct a concupiscent idea just to get a temporary fix for the situation. The problem is not enough resources, for the problem is our total evaluation of where we live at, goals, and the time to achieve them. Do we only think rationally on where the resources are going before they start to run out (not just low)? Also, how fast your resources are depleting is important to consider too. There are moments in life when thoughts pop up and nothing connects to where you can get out of that hard place of two rocks with no middle ground, which is worse than a rock and a hard place, but both are caused by past thinking. It is time to learn how to keep financial issues resolved, for all people need to always have $1,000 cash on hand. Yes, I was in a rough moment in life when nothing seemed to make sense and there was no one to help me out in the situation. Chaos, confusion, lack, and poverty all held me captive like my livelihood was stolen and all of what I went to school for was held for ransom.

It took the power of working with little until more came through, and this was done by reviewing everything that concerns money. At that time I was reviewing my elders' diaries and writings to see what they were up to before passing away, when a phone call changed things. That's when I submitted a love gift as seed for the ministry based on Matthew 6:38 where the Bible actually is correct on "Give and it shall be given back unto you." This dictates circulation of money leaving your hands and returning back with interest or more than before. When I did it from the heart, all things worked out well compared to giving just to look good for the people or a tax write-off. Nevertheless, there are times in life when we are encouraged to do the right thing and always question it. If this is you, then breaking the spell of issues named previously off your finances requires you to be in prayer and tithing. These are *some of the necessary steps* in getting out of the *unwanted comfort zone* of life to get full deliverance from the situation that you're in currently when it is not looking like its heading to accomplish goals for the future. In order to enjoy the future, we must learn from the past and make better choices in the present. If not, then we have plotted our own self-destruction by being the slackers, and the book of Proverbs speaks volumes about this issue of laziness which affects all things in life.

Don't let others mislead you when your first thought (instinct) versus the second thought (hesitation) leads you into an action that brings great results and advancement. You wind up missing the blessing and getting mad at the world because of your second thought when it's your own fault for missing your mark. For example, I was going to leave the house fifteen minutes early but waited to hear this one episode on YouTube before leaving out. My second thought was to leave early and go to the ATM, but I didn't, so I bumped into one of my neighbors who plugged me into a venue to make some money and the cost was timing and adhering to my first thought. Had I left earlier, I would have missed my opportunity to be invited to this venue in Brooklyn. Was I excited? Absolutely! And God gets the glory for exercising the extreme patience that is key, plus going with my instinct to wait before making a move forward. When things work out well because the right steps lead to prosperity and rewards are due to the work of your hands and the research that positions you for better going forward. Remember, the past never sees the present, unless you allow it, or travels into the future. You must make adjustments.

Patience is something our society is lacking, and some do have to deal with those who are always in a rush. But you don't need to contract this plague, for being impatient gets you not so good results. Yet we all have to deal with some ill-mannered behavior that comes along with the territory. For example, there was a person who was impatient on a check that they didn't receive and was losing his entire mind. They went to borrow money from all their "friends," but even their friends lacked to aid them. They didn't have credit cards, and their parents made demands on them for money which they owed them. They were flat-out broke with no resources lurking in the house. Instead of them being patient to get funds, they went four hours from their house only to get $20 and be ungrateful for getting it. Sadly they went through the same thing again, and I truly believe they were on a heavy drug for them to have weird problems with their second check from the second job problems. Face it, companies never want to have disgruntled employees especially when it comes to payroll. The problem was with them and extra-curricular activities that robbed them into poverty and despair. That behavior can be corrected and changed in time, depending if one wants to do it. Time and patience have their perfect work. In this instance, one must add patience to their faith to see God's promises come to pass in our lives (Hebrews 6:12). We all have to stand for a while on the Word of God before we see anything in this natural realm begin to change. Why? Because faith is a tool. We must apply this gift of the Spirit to operate it. Our faith will work when applied directly to the problem and the problem realize that it has to leave. That's why the fig tree is mentioned in Mark 11:14. When Jesus said to the unfruitful fig tree, "No man eats fruit of thee hereafter forever," on the outside nothing happened even though he said it by faith. But some time later, Peter called to Jesus to remind him of the "fig tree which thou cursed is withered away" (verses[18] 20–21). The tree dried up from the roots indicated that Jesus's faith went into operation the moment he released it. It was outwardly invisible, yet its effects were totally visible later on.

[18] Same chapter in the book of Mark.

Have You Ever Wished That Every Time You Prayed the Prayer of Faith, You Get Instant Visible Results?[19]

I remembered some time ago when some others and myself went to a healing service. The speaker was discussing things pertaining to faith, being well, and thinking better without the attachment of worry, stress, and despair or depression about debt and other matters related to life. In Family Law class, we discussed the topic of separation and divorce, which also can cause stress knowing that a relationship has gone broke, which technically is a bankruptcy. This can be stressful and can get so intense to where one can be ushered into an early grave. In Family Law class, we had jokes on a variety of topics presented, yet a few women in class had rebounded from the bankruptcy of the institution to divorce with unwanted bills from this terrible incident in their lives. Their former spouses got a lot and virtually left them with nothing more than pain in different areas that will wreak havoc for years to come. Then came the rebound out of debt and bankruptcy too. We all passed the class and moved on keeping caution in our mirror of life that keeps us aware of those who want the best for us versus the opposite. That is very important and will keep you with balance in both your personal and professional life. Most people overlook this very essential area of life. The wrong person in your life can be a catastrophe and the right person in your life can bring you joy, but bear in mind, there is no pop-out premade relationship man-or-woman package that we can buy. That means

[19] From the article *Prospering in a World of Cycles* by John Copeland.

there has to be more than just common ground and great sex, cooks good, looks good, and whatever other thing that may float through your head. Just a reminder, it does get lonely at the top, and many bosses and higher-ups in life want a smooth-flowing relationship that is not stressful and is beneficial to mental, financial, and physical health of both.

Now as for the service, it was not like we needed healing for our bodies. According to our eyes looking around the congregation, there was not a soul that was clutching a cane, walker, or was sitting in a wheelchair. It was healing for the other unspoken areas of concern. Yes, we all began the process of praying and asking to be forgiven for our sins and for mismanaging the things we were blessed with and more. As we all prayed, the entire congregation worshipped, praised, and stood in faith and believed for whatever we brought before the Throne of Grace and declared out loud that we were healed. The first step of the process reverses the situation because whatever happens in the spirit realm transpires later in the natural realm of our time. When we deployed our faith, it started displacing the sickness of finances and releasing healing to those who needed healing to their bodies. Over time many people's finances had gotten better and better, until eventually every aspect of lack was totally gone. That's the power of Jesus Christ and faith, in conjunction with knowing that the problem has been eradicated and now the doors of prosperity are open. But wait, in the world of finances, things tend to work out well too. The change happens gradually over time, especially when you know that you have been walking the floor every night, trying to figure out how this and that is going to get paid off. Monies for rent, tuition, books, carfare, and the list goes on. God wants you to prosper, and he said it in Jeremiah 29:11 that he wants to give you peace, prosperity, and longevity for growing older. I used to walk the floor at night to look over bills, and then one day I decided to just leave it in Jesus's hand. That's what I did. Also, I sowed a seed in one ministry, and from that day going forward, change came forth and finances started coming slowly at first. Then it started picking up, and then finally I was able to have a plan for beginning to stash a certain amount. See, everything runs in cycles—from the weather, to food chain, to economics.

One objective is to have a plan to stack anywhere from five hundred to one thousand dollars. It is a good start, and most people live paycheck to paycheck and don't have six months of anything to the side other than a mouth full of garbage and trolling through life. So to prevent that, we brace ourselves so that later on we have a stash for at least six months of rent or mortgage, plus another side stash of funds for reoccurring bills. Then work on having loose funds to do some light things much like a company having *petty cash* to work with during the slow times and light things needed unexpectedly for the office. Bear in mind: do not disturb heavy monies for the business or that you have unless you plan to return them back triple. This mind-set helps you and the new business or anyone during lean times until things get better. Yes, a plan is the *main tool* combined with steps to make things better and change what was not in place before to bringing everything correct and in full circle. Remember that Titus 1:2 requires you to speak by faith and keep focus on the Word, and yet he "calleth those things which be not as though they were" (Romans 4:17). See, when we stop focusing on the contrary circumstances and keep our eyes on the Word of God, circumstances change.

Like many people have been looking at the pandemic as wild and with fear, this is where one has to be creative and inventions come forth. We have to, for a moment, look away from our symptoms or from what our bank balance is saying, and we talk accordingly. As the Apostle Paul put it in 2 Corinthians 4:13; "We having the same spirit of faith, according as it is written, I believed, and therefore have I spoken; we also believe, and therefore speak." All it takes is remembering to live by faith, and whenever we see ourselves reviewing the problem all over again, just speak God's Word into our situation and forgive ourselves and those we may hold a grudge and try to walk in love. Yes, it's tough. Galatians 5:6 and Mark 11:25 command us to *forgive and love.* When you feel like holding a grudge against someone, it will hold up the blessing, miracle, and breakthrough that are needed to address things. Besides, this unhealthy stress can cause you to age quicker with health issues and die. Then because of the unrepentance of the sins, guess what's next? *Hell.* Also, living with a contrary mouth brings the same on your viewpoint, which will give negative results in your life and lead you to unwarranted social distancing. So I would focus on the good which is coming and that allows less stress. Keep in mind, in order to be not stressed, you want to be more blessed. Praise brings blessings and so does giving of your time, resources. Watch blessings come forth. Now your blessings not coming forth are based on a closed heaven spoken on in *Really???*, and its gateway is in the hands of angry God. Ask Cain.

If I was in your shoes, try not to repeat past hardships that didn't work toward prosperity. Seriously, avoid repeating the same financial clout mishaps. Or do you want to repeat any of life's lessons all over again? When I am told something that is beneficial, I seriously am obedient and receive the benefits. I recommend that you apply it in the stash programs suited to your lifestyle and watch how it works for you. Besides, one day I overheard a woman tell someone to stop talking negative about his or her situation while riding the train, and she was rough, stern, and didn't play. Now, men, we all know women like that and we do change our tune quickly! The tone of her voice relaxed because the person she was speaking to corrected their mouth and thoughts and began speaking words of faith. As she was getting off the train, I felt that as a reminder for a meeting in Coney Island.

You have to shake up your thinking from the way you used to do it and get with the new flow of how things are going to work for you. Bear in mind that when finances are depleted your pocket is sick and needs healing. In order to change, one must be receptive to it coming into full manifestation. Our president speaks those things as though they are when they are not in full order.[20] That's something that many people need to keep in mind going forward. Not just the church, but the society should be

[20] From Diamond and Silk when they were before a demo-cracked loaded Congressional hearing.

praying with selflessness for strength and then for others' success around you at the time of your roughest hardship and even when things are just cool. WATCH OUT! WATCH AND PRAY!

We live in a world where the Bible tells us, "While the earth remains, seedtime and harvest, cold and heat, summer and winter, and day and night shall not cease" (Genesis 8:22 Amplified Bible, Classic Edition). As long as we know one prime factor where fall is harvest time, winter is the time to be more inside and warm. Also, spring is the time of refreshing, planning, preparing, reevaluating our finances so that all the problems of the previous year will not be activated during this period of life going into the new year. In fact, it is best to keep in mind that when one plans and prepares for new things to matriculate, it is imperative to position oneself for success. It is during this time, one may stay in their current life cycle, but always focus on God, especially during the good times. Yet in these times we as humans get lazy and too self-absorbed within our comfort zone. The problem I have seen in many areas of my city is the fact that everyone has expensive phones and are always crying broke. It is the same as wearing two-hundred- to three-hundred-dollar sneakers and crying that you do not have any money. The last thing folks cry about is that they have money for their vices, but they don't have money to take care of their priorities. Since the economy is better, how is it one can travel without carfare roundtrip? Usury and covetous behavior has got to change as well; if not corrected in time, then you shall repeat having nothing. These behaviors and more have to change. If you want to stand up and be in a better position in life, change is required. But if you feel that a person is prospering pimping others through usury, those people do not prosper. Sadly it takes time, like a depression, when people have to reflect on all things that affect their life, especially when it's evil and has not helped you into prosperity (nor return with interest back to you). But during the social distancing, many people are in dire straits and really need help. Even those who use folks are in the need, and sadly they never had a viable plan going forward. They have desperation plan with plenty of folks that commit robberies, and that's not cool.

In tough times others get serious about the things of God. We start to dig through our notes within the Word and soar up spiritually for attacking the devil when we should have been preparing for the future instead of living for the moment. We all have done it from time to time. Some of us just overdo it and make it a habit of living off other people only to preserve their resources for the vices that do our bodies harm and wreak havoc financially. This is the "new" normal behavior that many use because they never really see the future, past their vices and struggles. When one can envision going to the store to restock their fridge and pantry, well, it's pretty parallel. Just like the chef can see the process where food transforms into being edible, it requires patience, vision, and most importantly, time! For the end product, we as people need to have unfettered curiosity and joy all the way until completion. For example, my cousin told me, "J, you have vision and can see what's coming for the future." That was a cool comment, although at the time it was spawned out of a discussion where my family in Harlem and I were celebrating the release of the first book and embraced great accomplishments especially when Black or Brown men are considered to be underachievers based on lack of exposure and proper influence that will allow better options to work with in life. But the interesting thing my cousin stated to me pertained to the fact that all of them are proud of me. Also, one of us doing great allows for others to do greater things too. For that is our family quote.

In life there are tough times in the economy as well as good times, but always keep your focus on doing more than what's right and maintain during challenging times. It is important to focus on the progress that God has allowed for you to obtain, maintain being healthy, and most importantly, you got up out of bed today. God and all that he has lined up for you is located in Jeremiah 29:11 and Psalm 122:7, because it empowers and employs Deuteronomy 28:1–7. It's like being a seed planted into the garden of life, for the days may bring good sunny days, rainy days, and the other elements. But through it all, we must maintain and keep focus on the good that is going to come forth from the seed of stashing for more than just a rainy day. God has blessed you greatly in so many ways that you think it's coming from this way but it comes from that way. The power of God, his Word, and your compliance with faith equals success! There are successful people who don't believe in God and others who worship idols who seem successful on the outside but lack peace on the inside. I want for you to have peace all the time, even in turbulence.

All cellular phone designers should have been working on new products for the market and look at the future to have new 5G phones instead of waiting until the network changed to actually begin work on a phone that can handle that network safely and securely. And it is that same way we need to always be focused on the future finances and pay attention to the trends of the present. This is why we must focus our strengths on staying ahead and don't be in the background. For success comes to those who actually are hungry for it and want better, like you want your 4G phone to be compatible with the network. The same thing with your finances; it must be flexible to suit your needs and expectations, like your phone. You need your finances to keep you in the land of doing well instead of facing problems or walking the floor at night. That is why many people I have talked with about precious metals seemed clueless about it. Yet they never or rarely back themselves up financially. That is not good. With metal in the stash, money comes to money and that paper money can go right in the stash. Follow the precious metals that will keep that law of attraction in check because we all know that money comes to money and you need this to be established and stay working in your life. Don't worry about the rainy day; just wonder about the day after.

That's why prior to writing this book, I did some reviewing with SD Bullion on YouTube to learn about precious metals. This, along with two other sources (plus comments), gave me confidence that metals will always maintain its intrinsic value, plus when I want to keep from being broke, this investment increases my future prospects while paper money runs to me because metals are money and having physical over digital metals benefits you, your family, and allows you to relax a bit more. Armed with reliable market date, I choose SD Bullion because all the comments basically are alert to the alarming printing of money. Plus it is great to know the past and present potential future standing of your investment. Like being in an affordable Wall Street without losses unless you have digital and no physical, then you lose big time. So for all of us not so rich folks, we need silver, and for those stepping into wealth gets both because the wealthy buy gold to stay rich, not to get rich. And with this statement, a friend of mine had made means to me that all of us who are not so rich should have silver to keep from being poor while our paper currency printing is causing inflation/poverty of our nation, which will soon leverage us out to a much "not discussed here" plan.

Keep the process of turning the topsoil of your life and add reading books, not the internet, to your diet. Write down your goals and aspirations, for without it, you can't position yourself to be comfortable with this next power move that I will share with you in order to not be broke.

Being Broke is a Sin and a Crime

The saying doesn't mean that you're rich. But it is a reminder to not speak yourself into poverty that will cause deficiencies in all healthy areas of your life over time. Remember earlier about the woman on the train conversation, when that word *broke* comes out your mouth? I stopped saying it, and saw all types of healing in all areas of my life. You can too!

Now, when people cry, "Broke," they are literally yelling "Fire!" in their pockets. They are saying that there is a fire of lack and poverty attacking the pockets. It is also letting the world know that that is what they are saying continually with their mouths and is what's in their heart and life. That's what is going to come to pass—financial suicide. Now, we all know that you wouldn't rob your company or your house. So speaking ill about your pocket does defeat your household from lining up to the period of progress. Remember, you live there! Why speak about being broke when that is financial suicide. Now, suicide is a sin and it's a crime if you hurt or cause someone else to die and you live. No good.

The next thing is that the person is saying, "God and his Word on being fruitful and multiple doesn't work for them."

The third thing that makes folks who utter those very words broke is due to not writing their goals down, which doesn't give them a clear path to step beyond broke. Why? Because without having vision translates to you not seeing yourself owning or being in a better position in life. So from out of the abundance of the heart the mouth speaketh; and out from this one set of actions causes points 1, 2, and 3 to coexist.

Sadly, some of these people are the same who criticize that paying tithes is wrong and giving to the poor is the same. They just told on themselves and basically don't have a tax write-off. That's the business side of the God. See Matthew 6:38. Now, all they are doing is stopping their own blessings because tithes are not always money; it could be time (two hours and forty-five minutes per day of spending time with the Lord, even while enjoying all activities of life going forward). And then there is whatever God puts on your heart to give. So whatever your gripe is, this season of struggle can and will soon pass. If you feel contrary, that's good because you should take a moment to share something with a person that doesn't have it. You will be *blessed*; trust me! I ask you to put your money where your mouth didn't go and find that old church and just give and see what happens during the week going forward.

Now, our next focus is to knock off all small slave masters via bills while stashing. I started my stash with seven dollars the other with twelve dollars and one more with twenty-five dollars, and to despise not the small beginnings. Because when you fail to plan, you plan to fail, and when you're grown, there's no time to fail.

I got an idea and needed to develop it into a plan. A plan that will lead to exposure will make a difference, absent being out of your comfort zone. This is where prosperity can begin and saturate your life going forward because the Bible showed me that "my people perish for a lack of knowledge: because thou hast rejected knowledge." Have a plan that accelerates your stash in order to have six months' rent and money for the phone bill and other things that will help out to stay ahead. Even in the bad times where everyone else is losing their job, you can always leave a card in the building where you live at and just leave an address for a job or temp agency for those unemployed. Anonymous help left for those whom you don't know brings a blessing back to you, like a promotion at your current spot and a raise or bonus.

If you want to be broke in the pockets, keep spending what you don't have. Your pocket will not recover with that reckless behavior like this because the outcome is a setback. You don't need that. And that is why it is highly important to know about investments that yield returns, interest from other markets, and review precious metals that can help tide you over too. A woman had a bar of gold bullion in the stash, and the town had no money. Well, when this one lady put that one gold bullion bar up for sale to obtain funding for her town to have a company therein, that was a life-changing event and a blessing.

Planning

One must brainstorm and write out a plan of action that can be achieved in time and add valuable success along the way; those unspoken victories and a mind-set to spend less and stash more, spend less and earn more, spend less and invest more, and spend less and live within your means! One must start somewhere for success to come forth. Trouble and uncertainty are a part of life, but we who are believers know for a fact who supplies all our needs. "And my God shall supply all your need according to His riches in glory by Christ Jesus" (Philippians 4:19).

Many scriptures do speak on the application, practical, and the tactile standing of knowledge gained from the Bible combined with having resources that helps you to live comfortably and help others around live better.

In the Bible, one of the names for God is El Shaddai, which means, "He who is more than sufficient to meet your needs." El Shaddai is God of all grace, God of miracles, and God of all supply. When Abraham and his wife, Sarah, were in their old age, they knew him as God of the impossible. As promised, God worked a miracle and gave the couple a son despite their old age, and there was no Viagra and both were in their nineties. This is serious, and many people wonder why they are not blessed. Doubt can constrict your flow of progress. The keys to life and success are based on a few key principles that have been developed in the world from the Old Testament to the New Testament and set forth in a clear depiction of *checks and balances*. It is these consistent checks of the Old Testament that many people seldom pay attention to certain key portions pertaining to the life of finances.

Many times in life, parents prevent their children from getting into all sorts of problems and other unforeseeable things. It is this godly wisdom that allows saints to know integral rights or wrongs, and the Lord Jesus Christ always provides guidance into clarifying affairs which breed success. All that is remembered is the necessary tools that are needed to prove that you can advance to a new level. These are the tools from earlier, discussed along with other portions of valuable nuggets. It is these measures that define:

Plot. An idea that you choose to do better for the success of the idea and position yourself to help others if necessary. Use notes, conversation on various points that bring growth, and other viable methods of love that allow you to lay out a plot. Further review the plot of Jeremiah 29:11 which grows into a developed plan.

Plan. A strong component of sowing and reaping. The results bring better stream of income which allows one to circumvent being the tail and only remain the head going forward. Being the tail in life does not allow you to get ahead due the danger of your credit score, acceptance for loans, new cars, homes, and anything that propels you to being in a better position in life. Bad credit scores and lack of resources will pose a serious problem. Also, the problem which was caused by the Cleoptocratic Clown Posse (China's CCP) and the extreme gross negligence of the world's worst health mob is one that God is going to deal with as we check ourselves and help those close by who need masks, gloves, and food to eat. Helping our neighbors is biblically sound, and there is always a blessing that abounds forth thereafter.

For example, when most people think to save money for a rainy day, but they don't really consider the prospects of the day after the rainy day. This gives rise to why many of us have to change that one mind-set that being in a better position to prosper and not be desperate or in dire straits is vitally important and requires discipline to maintain all things accumulated. Most importantly, "Trust in the Lord with all thine heart, lean not unto thine own understanding" (Proverbs 3:5 KJV). This one scripture has been on one business owner's answering machine since Moses held the Ten Commandments in his hand and came off the mountain. Although you might chuckle, guess what, this one small business owner has helped many people obtain funds in the north of about over more than $40 million dollars and growing. Yeah, they have had a few challenges within the life of the business, and that has led many to seek both counseling and prayer from business owners who are believers and who know that the Bible and some of the more than seven hundred scriptures on finance combined with faith will always bring success.

This success *Prevents* our actions of not being in debt, not having investment, no emergency, no stash, and no backup stash plus zero accounts and no flexibility to your broke pocket. The holes therein allow money to evaporate. When we pray and stand on the Word, these resources will stand through tough times because you have prepared for them to be highly essential. Unlike debt, consolation and bankruptcy counselors want you to list all your debts; that is good. I want for you to pray over all your debts, and whatever words the Lord Jesus gives to you to say, then say them and put those bills down and declare, "VICTORY IN JESUS'S NAME!" over all your bills and step boldly into today and do not stress over the bills or what did not get paid. They will be paid eventually. Bear in mind that not too many people would ever share with you about having a stash or any of the abovementioned tools that will keep you from being thirsty every time someone pulls money out of their pockets versus you looking and being happy about the next person having funds. Plus, you take the strain off your household and the stress rolls right off you. Water to a duck is how stress rolls away from you and your household. The projection in life is to have the financial grip on hand because your purchase of this book kept you from going to a debt counselor, bankruptcy lawyers, and then to court. Then think seven or ten years without being trusted with a loan is a problem if you truly want to pimp a bank and all parties get paid from this financial gain, including you. This is not a get-rich-quick scheme but a simple plan to prep your finances and other things.

The one subject that we talked about in school and in several men's group discussions was poverty and lack. It was also discussed in-depth at one church service that these are two twin demons that everyone faces.

Lack and Poverty

Yes, these twins do have a bite on households when stress is high and money is low. When the economy is doing bad, crime in all forms goes up. The convoluted thinking and disbelief that budgets do not work is ignorant and shows how they treat bread, loot, clout, bag. It will lessen their financial grip which technically shows us that their intent with money is displaced and may not be on the same level as your own and makes their views dangerous enough to impact finances horribly. That's why most people do not have much of anything and always want what you have. We need to break away from those mind-sets. That's not healthy, and it only goes downhill fast. People who are living for today and don't care about tomorrow are totally shameful. They don't realize that they're lax in reviewing where or what to do in order to avoid using people and living a covetous life. These are the desperate people one must be aware of in all aspects of life, for they plot, scheme, and will attempt to rob, steal, kill, and continue with their practice until stopped—a practice which is opposite yet breakable. Triumph over dealing with these two creepy best friends who are the frontrunners of stinky thinking and feeding the vices.[21] In fact, it took me not just to hear it but to exercise it. A practice that was spoken in *Gold-Digger Christians* and *Really??? (The Amendment).* This exercise, which is not hardly practiced in secret and reluctantly, are not adhered to even when it comes to their vices and unnecessary wants which leave them with temporary satisfaction and an unsolved addiction.

[21] Drinking, smoking, using drugs (without prescription and illegal ones), using vape, and a few other vices or bad habits that can get the best of budget and prevent the goal of stashing without pressure.

There are annoying statements always made by folks even when they are not: *"I'm broke,"* "This place is broke," and so on. These are big problems because those words breed power for your day going forward, and when you speak against God's people on this matter, you are impacted quickly. When a person keeps saying those things and living their life that way, they will remain broke too. They never will be in a better position until their mind-set and heart change. A friend of mine had told me that and others when we were younger, being that we did hang out with all types of people. They stated, "All your friends have no jobs or no income to help pay for things when hanging out. That means that you are as broke as them." And it never dawned on me that association is as contagious as the problems that others face. Trust me on that.

Remember, when you have a network of individuals that stand with you on all the positive achievements that matter in your life, your haters only give you energy to succeed and God does give you the rest. This means, you got off your butt and did something constructive realizing through an epiphany; you have value in the works of your hands when given the opportunity for going to pursue upgrades within your life or the lives of others that you interact with breaks poverty and lack. How? Read on.

When you speak to a neighbor, who you're cool[22] with, and have ties with them outside of living in the same building, this communication allows advancement toward a new job, cars, places to live, girlfriend, boyfriends, (future) spouses, new business endeavors, and the list goes on.

Keep in mind that prayer provides for you to be focused on the things that really matter and would allow your life to be a billboard of success for others to see God's hand in your life. It is extremely important to always put God first and foremost, and all things that concern you will be addressed without stress. There is no magical style, scientific formula, or certain method in approaching the throne of grace to get the results that you need. It is necessary but not mandatory to have two or three prayer partners that can touch

[22] Because of favor according to Psalm 5:12, "It surrounds you like a shield."

and agree on the things which concern you. Because the Word of God states, "When two or three are gathered in his name, he is there in the midst." These recipes of success are to make moves in life. Whether you believe in God or not, whether you are a backslider or holier than thou, and whatever your background is in life, these tools do work; you just have to work it out in your own situation and life circumstances. You want money to work for you and go further than where you're standing today? Well, it takes practice, makes permanent, and uniquely brings GREAT RESULTS! Yesterday and today, people behind the scenes can't stand poor people, and the Bible has always stated, "The poor you have with you always," so they're not going anyway by force or otherwise. So when we see the poor, WE should really try not to look down on them. If we have a carryout bag of food that is a bit much or can afford to give a meal, then do so, but don't post it on social media. There are plenty of reasons of why some people are poor and others are not. I recall from scripture one night when I came from study hall at two in the morning and saw the entire area had transformed into a homeless zone. Then this scripture came upon me: "The poor ye shall have with you always." That was more than enough reason to know that it's going to be on this earth as long as humans coexist, but there are some valid points as to why some people are poor. A book I read in college called the *The War on Poverty* stated, "We throw money at poverty and it was to the tune of $5 million and years later $50 million was the real number, but it does nothing to lift people out of poverty." Most just checked out of life and exist day by day.

Another pointer is, many who are poor are so because of *lack of knowledge,* so they need to learn to get their way out of debt. Those are people waiting for someone to knock on their door with a check or something to get them motivated into nothing. According to Dr. Leroy Thompson Sr. in *Money Thou Art Loosed,* "When you loose money using your authority on the earth, I will loose the ability to cause that which you said to come to pass." In order for the situation to change, giving is more than a tax refund. It can be also the attitude to how one deals with resources that has to change. People can sense a person who has a beggarly attitude versus one that wants to get their hands dirty and put in work. There are times in life when we have a poor thought process. This thought process affects all things as well as our self-esteem. The Bible states, "As a man thinketh." This reflects that a man's or woman's countenance—coupled with the actions, lifestyles, and choices—impacts other major areas of life. Being poor is not just a state of mind, for it can be living in poverty of evil thoughts to getting out of poverty, only to transform illegal evil gains appearing like prosperity. And the gains are short-lived, whereas if they were introduced to the standards equated to Booker T. Washington standard—which allowed for the establishment of education in Tuskegee, where men or women of color received an education that gave them more latitude towards success that is legal and all who achieved it shall be blessed continually. Address things necessary in preventing all within your circle to not slip into the abyss of lack and poverty. This will work when you work it out, team style! It also helps to prevent poverty and living in desperation. Yes, we all have some poor thoughts that arise to the level of stinking thinking, but it doesn't mean we have to incorporate this ingredient that brings harm and wrong choices, affecting your destination can be devasting. Furthermore, in order for things to change, Luke, in chapter 8, speaks on substance. The reason why we have poor thoughts is due to lack of positive substance. There is an old saying that says, "Be careful of what you eat." That applies in all things. Reading, listening, smelling, tasting, and touching are part of the five senses, and what they are equal to is the everyday things we do in life. If a person doesn't know how to handle money, then they are forced to deal with a situation where the truth really comes out and if they don't pass the test of life, then they will repeat it all over again!

Very few know this wrongful thought process can be painful and have a stench to the likes of *stinking thinking,* which hurts and breaks up more friends and families than all violent crimes combined and yet it is allowed to fester when an offer or presentation to get something for nothing comes about. The one who does not know that this is a scam will be burned for more than their bread. It burns the ego and hurts those who take things on face value. My uncle used to say, "You can't con an honest man unless they are about con themselves." That is what stuck with me going forward and I share that with many when we talk seriously about stashing and stacking. Yet stinky thinking does hurt and destroy people into being desperate and not optimizing their real potential and only want to deal with instant gratification, like a car, house, something material that shows you're in debt or trouble. These were obtained from stinky thinking, and it will hurt when the cards come crashing down. When this hurt affects a lot of people, like the number of people killed with a .22-caliber bullet, then change needs to take root quickly. Stinky thinking and poverty are two things that need to be considered seriously when you want to make moves going forward. Let's begin. When you go to work or back to work, there are all sorts of conversations, but you don't get involved. The oldest trick in the book to see who is an ally is for people to approach you. But if a person welcomes you into the gossip group, remember, don't say a word. Just listen and get a feel of who are the backward cheerleaders, a.k.a. the haters, and last but not the least, the nonworking or underworking hater and brown-noser (nosy person). These are necessary characters to be mindful of who are the eyes, ears, and your allies in the company you work at. However, there is one other thing to be on point about tardiness: the time you want to take a power nap. Yes, there are jobs so boring that a pillow is a major help to do a terrific job, but the goal here is to keep you with employment and of course you keeping track of how much time you need for qualifying for unemployment and possible food stamps as well. After all, it's your tax money (mine too), but this is your final backup plan in case anything happens at your new job. Look at both food stamps and unemployment depending on the state. Hopefully, you will not need to go that route and can proceed to better pay.

Next is the crazy concupiscent thoughts that if voiced would not be too cool at all, and depending on what ill-minded thought was spoken, your day will surely be a regretful one. Another thing that is stealing time, leaving items around for you to either keep them, turn them in, or bring them to the lost and found. Personally, if something is left behind, bring it to a supervisor and also take a picture with your phone just in case. This saved a coworker of mine who saw a huge pile of cash in the car. I took a picture of it so that no one can steal it or anything crazy shy of having a nice day at work would be a problem. People set people up all the time, and integrity is one of the major components that is hardly ever *stressed* to adhere to because those who perform it are looked at as outcasts. The time we have quality versus nefarious ways, where jealousy coupled with stinking thinking is a problem that allows a whole host of other things to manifest. See, the Bible states, "Out of the abundance of the heart, the mouth speaks." This portion of scripture is presented because it reminds us to check the things that are spoken out of disgust of not having enough which can impact our finances and bring unwanted change in our circumstances. This is not always right and legal; in law this is called enrichment, which is totally different from entitlement.

See, "Those obsessed with money, hold on to it, they don't make it move. That's what makes them interesting." Because these are the same people who scheme and scam to obtain just about everything they own. The same energy asserted could have a person own things of substance that will last far longer than the things obtained dishonestly. A person can obtain something from another person, place, or institution (this includes homes of married couples, relationships, not just limited to finances). And yes, you read obtaining somebody that is not yours rightfully and legally, which is correlated to abduction or kidnapping and in our society is a crime. But was it a crime when a person met up with you and you both started socializing alone together? It's not a crime figuratively, but financially it is, because you are allowing yourself to be derailed and one you cannot afford to slip while in the midst of a great stack-up of finances. Remember, drinking or doing drugs requires time, money, energy, transportation, food, and most importantly, it deducts from your rest too.

The last two reasons why people don't have money is, the ones that believe and trust in God should not be trying to get their financial increase from gambling, scamming social programs, and scamming people out of funds or food. This addictive behavior has torn up more families. These are they who lack authority over their giving.

They haven't been able to fully trust the Lord to get it back to them when he asked them to give. They haven't mastered the part called expectation and reaping which will put into circulation of reciprocity that brings interest when it returns. And these are those who say they are Christian in name. Take my advice and trust God!

Another thing is, people are rarely thankful; they are extremely greedy and possess an attitude of the-more-I-make-the-more-I-take syndrome. When they increase, they forget about the Lord and all those good people who advanced them. They forget that he is the giver of every good and perfect gift (James 1:17) and that he is the one who gives the power to get wealth (Deuteronomy 8:18). They get into what I call paying-the-world-and-tipping-the-Lord syndrome. The Bible asks the question, "Will a man rob God?" (Malachi 3:8). People who rob God when they withhold tithes and offerings from the church and from the work of God do see a return on their finances. It is not good, and I will leave it like that unless you journey into Malachi 3:8–12 and Matthew 6:38, the law of giving and reaping. They do a wonders when it's adequately applied, and when it's not, then it shows too.

How do we change this mind-set? Is this mind-set yielded to the ordinances of God? This is where it begins to change, and being poor will be a memory and a reminder that we should decide to turn around. (Like the woman to whom the angel said, "Keep going and do not look back," in Genesis before the destruction of Sodom and Gomorrah. She decided to be disobedient just before her breakthrough and she looked back and her life changed from living to a pillar of salt.) Well, the aspect of looking back to review the past is not always good. For those actions may not be as detrimental as the above, but can go through weird changes that can hurt in more ways than one.

These are times we need to make a call for prayer. Thus, making the good moments and overcoming the bad ones. Yes, we all have good memories and those are what keep our hopes, dreams, and personal factors grounded. But we have bad ones too. What do we do? Do we call on Jesus to help us, or do we just pick up the phone and call someone that may be able to take our mind off the issue? Do we just cope with the rough feelings at this time? What about those who have no one to help him or her? What are they supposed to do? School told me that counseling will help and, combined with prayer, will bring things around quicker. Well, in times like those issues discussed above, a confession to friends and Jesus Christ is necessary to be in grace, mercy, and moreover to have help. We all have stinky thinking. Some are acts of violence, others are more sexual in nature; however, we all have to work on curbing the stinky thinking and seek Jesus's face for help with this wrong mind-set. (I did it for both good and bad thoughts.) For Jesus Christ will give you all the necessary components and friends to help his beloved win against this area of problems. Romans 8 speaks on renewing your mind, which allows you to hear the Holy Spirit guiding you to lead a successful life. According to Jeremiah 29:11, you are the "apple of his eye." Bear in mind, all these good factors presented are serious enough to apply scripture and how it is not conducive to be poor. The Bible shares with us that a man, woman, or child is always blessed for the *works of their hands.* So stop living under the curse of law and put yourself in direct lineup of being blessed with grace, prosperity, and success. For a person who lives under the curse of the law cannot live a life of liberty and blessings; something is totally wrong.

When we all look forward to having a better life and for our loved ones, true success is reviewed through one hand of progress which breeds prosperity. After watching a young lady who mentioned "The second time, you're getting better," Tamira Johnsen shared in her video that her friend had opened three businesses. Each time it was better produced, and most importantly she had the ability to put the entire process for progress in order to step into enjoyment of prosperity.

Prosperity

Jeremiah 29:11 says, "'For I know the plans I have for you,' declares the Lord, 'plans to prosper you and not to harm you, plans to give you hope and a future.'"

Understand that success is based on prospering, and when you prosper, you and those connected to you *win*! The good part of prospering is knowing that you have great health, for without it, one cannot go forward to achieve each and every goal that they set forth to do. This very scripture is listed above to make you realize that having a stash is not illegal. Some people want you to be broke, and others want for you to succeed. No matter how much stress is going on in life, to work with your hands allows you more blessings that bring things full circle. That is what a blessing is supposed to do—not just to be there temporarily but to establish you into a level that even your haters will not be able to deal with the fact that God has blessed you to be ahead of them. Once ahead, don't fall or get cocky either. Just keep making moves in humility and integrity when haters come out of left field with wrong facts and other wrong intentions. Just ignore them!

These very jewels of stacking money actually put me into a position to be ahead in rent until February 2020. Then this Franken Germ came forth and killed a lot of people of various backgrounds in my city, leaving my town with issues that may result in the fulfillment of prophecies spoken by David Wilkerson and others. So, doing the math going forward, you have my secret on how to stack and stash it. And the plan is not limited to the funding that is listed. It works with anything, and you may have to get your hands dirty to make things work on many levels. What do I do with my time, or what can I stash more with my stash? Or is there a project that I can get my hands dirty working on and not looking at the accumulation of wealth? Enjoy the fact that you live within your means, and that is super. And the ability to be a steward over what you were blessed with; and trust me, whether you believe in God or not, a power greater than you has gotten you out of bed this morning. For without health, wealth means nothing without your family, team, and any others that stood by you to endure all the changes of growth. That is when you give a sigh and say, "Thank you!".

Economic Power

True economic power comes when you admit that there is a financial problem and you're willing to learn how to do better without having it cost you later on in life. That's the first step to addressing your problems. "Therefore, as ye abound in everything, in faith, and utterance, and knowledge, and in all diligence and in your love to us, see that ye abound [increase greatly] in this grace also" (2 Corinthians 8:7). This fulfills Jeremiah 29:11 and allows the entire prospects of Genesis 12:3 to manifest within your life because you came to the first step in growth. That first step of growth is the moment you admitted a problem, and now because of that, watch how God can help you out when you ask him. It is much like AA, NA, or SA. All have the component that humble participants do share with the community that admitting is the first honest step to a clean life. It applies in the world of finances too. You cannot keep asking for a blessing and not doing the right things with the funds you have, which is not correct living. You must change your mind-set when dealing with resources. Remember that if you are not budgeting, stashing with discipline, or stashing in case of emergency, then you have a problem. And sadly, you have a mind-set for failure. But this can change, and it takes time, patience, and diligence to make it happen. Have little to no dependency on plastic money that is not yours but a loan. Remember that debt is the slave master, and in order to not be affected by it, I implore you to apply these basic tools to not be stash-less and resource-less. Don't be a slave to debt!

Let's say you have a bad financial situation and never knew or trusted Jesus or anyone to help you with getting out of the rut but saw a coworker or classmate who actually is blessed and everything is always fresh. You never saw them when they were going through the season of trials, hell, and Jesus took a lunch break and the devil took control of their life. And you have been evil, not resting, and everything you tried failed! You even tried suicide, and that didn't work. Until now, you've been thinking about it, worrying about it constantly, day in and day out. You've been going to bed worrying about it and then picking it up the moment you wake up. The important thing to realize is that you've created a habit of thinking about the whole situation. What caused it? What's the answer? Searching your mind for the answers is like searching through a file cabinet over and over but not finding the file you're looking for. Why do you do this and not have peace?

It's not in there! The answer isn't in your mind; it's in your born-again spirit because the spirit of God, who knows everything, and his love guide you (1 Corinthians 2:16). Just learn to confess your sin and to seek first the kingdom of God and all things shall be added unto you. As you cast the care of the problem over onto him, standing on the financial promises in His Word, say this: "I see, Lord Jesus, that you are my care taker. Philippians 4:19 boldly declares that you shall supply *all* my needs according to your riches in glory. Now, I boldly declare by faith that I do not, and will not, carry the care and anxiety of this any longer. I repent of the sin of worry and unbelief, and I refuse to touch this thing in my thought life any longer." It works best when you do all this before taking communion. Then bind the devil with the mighty weapon of the name of Jesus; the blood for the Word is powerful! (Even if you don't attend a church service regularly, at least go in the beginning of the month and see what happens next; I challenge you.)

The moment you catch yourself thinking about that care again, cast down that imagination and the thought of it immediately! Say, "I don't touch that. That's no longer my care, so that's no longer my thought!" Don't tolerate even the smallest thought of it anymore! And don't allow anyone who knows this situation to discuss the bad side of things. Let's focus on the victory! You are preparing for a victory and cancelling out stress of worry. The thoughts of the problems will become fewer and further apart until you'll finally realize they're gone! And you practice not worrying going forward, for worrying does not allow for you to enjoy. Psalm 122:7 tells us that we are to have peace within "thy walls." This means that your home life should line up with that scripture. If not, then you need to pray and prepare for some house cleaning. I'll close with a scripture, but now it will take on a new and more powerful meaning for us.

> Be careful [anxious] for nothing; but in everything by prayer and supplication with thanksgiving let your requests be made known unto God. And the peace of God, which passeth all understanding, shall keep your hearts and minds through Christ Jesus. Finally, brethren, whatsoever things are true, whatsoever things are honest, whatsoever things are just, whatsoever things are pure, whatsoever things are lovely, whatsoever things are of good report: if there be any virtue, and if there be any praise, think on these things. Those things, which ye have both learned, and received, and heard, and seen in me, do: and the God of peace shall be with you. (Philippians 4:6–9)

Just remember to exchange your old thoughts of the care and worry with good and wonderful thoughts and praise to God. However, you can read this book until you wear out the pages, but if you don't commit to making changes, the things I've shared with you throughout the pages will not work on its own. You do have to put effort into it, and yes, it does require sticking to the plan and being disciplined when the time comes for you to splurge or get your "bling on." Do it with style and keep this in mind: "When you spend money, someone always profits; [but] when you save it up, you are the only one who benefits. That may make you happy temporarily, but you would never know the joy of those around you who feel happiness as well."[23]

---

[23] Control, Episode – Season 1 – Conspiracy: Date – unkown.

Know why successful people practice insulation and isolation, but embrace the downtime when they're alone. There was a show I was watching where they spoke on why successful people hide. The comment from Nice Shot stated, "Why do successful people hide?[24] To keep the leeches off." May I drop the fact that a few rappers from my old neighborhood in Queens moved from there because of peace of mind and they wanted not to be in a situation with irrational people especially when you're feeling good or coming in twisted or touch-up. The other reason, which Ryan posted, was "The worst part is the 'friends' who come out asking for loans. It made me get off social media for good." Sport 3504 commented, "It ain't that people don't like nice things, they just don't want you to have them if they can't obtain them." All these comments I pulled are exactly why people who are successful are always on the *Da Low.*

If you want to get to the level of where you want to be in life, be serious enough to work countless hours and stay up countless nights in order to make sure your plan of life and success is valuable for you and your family. There is a psychological dynamic that if the past family members and yourself work and try to save loot, later on your child will do the same. They will be repeating the same things that keep us free from struggling without a stash, investments, gold, silver, and MRE food.

These actions are the proponent of synchronicity where the past, present, and future are interconnected, and it's bigger than money.

[24] Grant Cardone YouTube channel. 2019. "Why Do Successful People Hide?" Nice Shot, Sport3504, and Ryan, thank you for your comments. They are on point.

Performance

In this area of performance, one can see how faith with works begins the process to flourish good fruit in your current situation. This action opened up the many doors of blessings in my life and in the lives of others. However, all the blessings did not come overnight. Remember, "The blessings of the Lord breed stress in both the natural and the supernatural." A prayer warrior had shared that with all of us, and all these years I see it confirmed each and every time. Also, another thing that a different prayer warrior had shared with me was when the Lord Jesus Christ is about to bless you, time seems to move fast to obtain it and slow once it comes into your possession. These are things that are ongoing *now*! And this will continue until Jesus comes back, along with miracles, blessings, and deliverance that has not been seen since the dawning of time, way before the start of the tribulation, the final days of mankind. And you don't want to be here for that either!

In further discussion on the topic of performance, I bring you the facts that we as people need to stop putting our dreams to the side and cease settling for crumbs and step up into what we are supposed to do, which is *Living the Dream,* first written in BVOV, May 2012.[25]

Some people may say that everything is too expensive to live my dreams, and there are so many disgruntled people chasing finances just to keep a roof over their head, food in the fridge, and just to blatantly survive. It can be a challenge and at times overwhelming, but we make it happen and it's not by our will, but by thine will. So in order to activate this component of life, we must have our things

[25] Gloria Copeland. 2012. *Living the Dream.* BVOV.

in order before we can bring them out for the performance. For prior planning does prevent poor performance comingled with prayer and preparation. How are you going to get a stash just depending on food stamps to come? Why do some people act nice only to ask you for money? This is all performance, and the difference of theirs versus yours means success without undermining your integrity and cheapening yourself. See, a CEO and business owner used to tell me, "When you go to the client's house, you are cheapening yourself." He didn't know that I was writing a book on the train, learning new things, and sharing the love to others. Who cheapened themselves? The one stationary or the one who used time to benefit them for the future where one has to prepare for the performance of a lifetime. That's your success that no one sees, because they can't see the future. Not even a palm reader is close to accurate. The only person who can show you your good future is God! He has the power to do so. That's why I share Jeremiah 29:11 so much in my writings, because I am evoking the power of your success by my faith joining with yours through Matthew 18:19, "Touch and agree," which means no junk, only real-deal prosperous things that will bring God glory and change your situation. See, when I was reading about living the dream, it dawned on me that all the things that we're going through around the avenues of struggle and doing-okay boulevard is a war to secure comfort in our lives. The battlefield of finances is dragged from one's hands into the stash. It seems like a battle to go from no stash into having a serious stash that keeps you from being in the ATM's, having people watch your money that you spend at the store, and most importantly, keeping you from being a victim. Yes, it keeps you from having your info stolen and other things which are important not to be compromised. These tools are necessary for you to remember every day when you get up and start your day. In addition, pray and make moves.

You are called to get up every morning and live out the dream conceived by God himself which lines up with Jeremiah 29:11, Psalm 122:7, and Genesis 12:3 (on being blessed). These scriptures are tools and remedies to what you do not currently possess. But if you want to know what that dream involves, all you have to do is read the Bible. It's all there—from Genesis to Revelation. Now as long as you keep that in mind, the next thing of which we are created to do on earth is to be fruitful and multiply and subdue the earth. Genesis 1:26 commands such. Understanding fruitful, multiply, and subdue the earth is what we as humans are supposed to do and on a more intrinsic view of the first of the three.

Being fruitful is the totality of anything that you have—gift, calling, passion, and dream. The beginning for fruitfulness is the seed of the abovementioned aspirations that allow you to live a powerful good life no matter what the circumstances around you may tell your five senses. In fact, being fruitful involves more than just having children. It is key to helping others and being a pillar in the times of challenges. Yes, these changes come from when we are proactive. Stop letting our current vision tell us things are hopeless and stop listening or believing the news when they share with everyone wrong things that are contrary to your blessings and livelihood. Yes, there are things that will not be reported since public emotions may get razzed causing all types of problems that a society don't need. Got it?

Another example: When the tax laws had changed, the second year the news reported that everyone is going to owe money, and it was not true for all my clients and I. In fact my new clients didn't owe a dime to the IRS and in fact many came off with double the money from which their past return may be $2,000 and this one is $4,000. It all comes from the application of three things in understanding the tax laws of today are a combination of the Bush tax combined with the elimination of the HR 3990 Affordable Health Care Mandate coupled with our president's wittiness in dealing with numbers. Technically before the tax law went into effect, the embassy was moved from Tel Aviv to Jerusalem, which was the act of Genesis 12:3, "I bless those who bless thee." It was a blessing for the president and the USA for the embassy to be moved, and that power move he did allowed all those who were voting against the tax laws to actually vote for them instead. Yes, junk was talked about it, but everyone that gets about $1,600 per dependent is not chump change. If it is chump change, tell all those who needed to make something happen with the extra $600 to give it back. If not, then it has a job to do. So when a bill has its hand out for payment, then it's not "crumbs" as one Congress official stated. Because those very crumbs defeated a few creeps named bills and subtraction of lack in the financial strength, which in short time it gets reversed to becoming stronger. Also, when we realize our standing in life, things work out a lot better, especially when God places right people in the pathway. It helps our lives. Even if they are a pretty woman or a good-looking dude, you should not sleep with everyone that comes in your life, nor should they be pimped either. There are reasons why this is stated. This is due to the mind-set of our current society and being hit on after a job interview by a dude, who was the interviewer. At that time I ignored him and should have reported it, but I left that in God's hands because some fights are not truly necessary to pursue. In the world of employment, there seems to be an overwhelming presence of lustful intentions and weird concupiscent mind-sets which are counterproductive to where you want to be in your new employment or business for growth coupled with what God has placed in your dreams, visions, and discussions with mentors, along with the people that help you not be lazy or take from you. For without mentors and others that have your best interest, one cannot achieve the goals without a team that has love, advice, and true success stories that bring achievement through *discipline*. Once you have achieved the first goal, keep going on. Write a goals list and check on it to make sure that you complete it. Once you complete the goals list, then get started writing another one.

Also, learn to dodge the snares of life. The snares can be lack, spending money on things that are short-term or dead investments, or damaged merchandise. People are happy, but they never really get a chance to enjoy the new raises, bonuses, and perks of the new economy, which is a problem. Now we all know that this economy has been hot ever since President Trump announced he was running and got elected. I want for many of you who read this book to know that the Dow is going to be fifty thousand points. It was stated for some time that there will be marital law and to have things set to the side. Well, based on the social disturbance, hopefully we can get back to life without anyone declaring pandemic, which is a medical declaration of martial law and can last for the first time up to a year or more with the whole nation under curfew. And if full martial law was imposed, It would place the nation under five years sequestered in their houses. That's why you should not laugh at people who tell you to put something extra to the side. Prepare to have food and all necessary items on hand for the next time we have to social distance. You don't want to look like the hurricanes Katrina and Sandy crowd. Also, become more independent and learn to grow food, sew, and other skills that should be taught to our current generation so that they can truly survive. Learn to get out of the habit of looking for someone to bring you something. This translates into you panhandling your friends or family. Do not allow laziness and other unproductivity to rob them of opportunities for resources. The Bible states, "Poverty and shame come to him who refuses instruction and correction, but he who heeds reproof is honored," (Proverbs 23:18 AMPC). Hustling people is stealing especially when you can get a job or work for a company, sweep a floor, mop, and run errands for people. Always stack something to the side for the days after the rainy day, and remember that every September is National Preparedness Month for all of us to stash something that can keep you and your house stabilized.

It's biblical and our Federal and local governments advised everyone every September, because it is National Preparedness Month that keeps your family in good shape and means that "*A good man* [or woman] *leaveth an inheritance to his* [or her] *children's children*" (Proverbs 23:22). Look, whether you like President Donald J. Trump or not, it's your personal business, but the prime concern while he is in office is for you to stack more and put it in the stash and not in the bank. Get items that can help you instead of panic stocking. That is why I am relaying a strong message from my rich classmates and wealthy mentors. Acquire at least more than five hundred silver coins and bullion. It's necessary to have silver and gold so you are able to eat and live well. If not for you, then for your family. Install wealth into your bloodline ASAP.

For a coin is money, and bullion is in block form and is wiser to use for transactions just like coins. If someone suggests to put money into diamonds, its good; but you would have to convert it into paper currency. Furthermore, having gold and silver is relative to biblical and historical currency. That's why I personally think it's a better bargaining chip for extra food where you don't deplete your primary stash or have a leech try you. Time will come when true hardships will hit this nation pursuant to the scriptures on famine not just in the book of Revelation. It is also mentioned in Matthew 24:7, Mark 13:8, and Luke 21:10–11. All of these show that famines shall come.[26] Let's take a look below.

> For nation shall rise against nation, and kingdom against kingdom: and there shall be famines, and pestilences, and earthquakes in diverse places. (Matthew 24:7)

For nation shall rise against nation, and kingdom against kingdom; and there shall be earthquake in divers places, and there shall be famines and troubles: these are the beginning of sorrows. (Mark 13:8)

Then said he unto them, nation shall rise against nation, and kingdom against kingdom. And great earthquakes shall be in diverse places, and famines, and pestilences, and fearful sights and great signs shall there be from heaven. (Luke 21:10–11)

All the scriptures above speak about this one event that will happen and will continue to progress more and more as time goes on. These scriptures will be fulfilled and the rapture will happen. Then shortly afterward, there will be no rain for *seven years*, and the problems will begin when it happens in North America. So keep in mind that this book is designed to help you get around many problems and provide surety of tools for you, for your family, and for your friends. Have some items to trade or aide your neighbors (if within an apartment building)[27] without being a victim of a crime. A must to have some level of security on hand, better to have it and not need

---

[26] The story of Joseph in the book of Genesis.

[27] If you're in the city instead of being in a small town, or vice versa, one can trade or barter.

it than to need it and not have it. However, the goal of life is not to stress over your present but to recognize where you're at spiritually, physically, mentally, and financially. All these specific items will enable you to maneuver through the growth streams once discipline is applied. In a nutshell, you will never say again that you're broke ever again. However, you may state differently at times that you are on low funds. God be my witness that he is going to make his power move for you to be better and to exceed abundantly.

Take the specific step of looking at your now, be prepared for obtaining your next, and think like most people when they go for a loan. They check all four or three credit reporting agencies for their report. But one thing that is totally overlooked is when looking at your credit scores from all three or four credit agencies, add them up and divide by three or four, because the true number of your credit score will be the answer. Once division is completed, then you can make your next monies accordingly to help you stack and stash better and bigger. If you have bad credit, then you can get a secured First Premier Credit Card. Just open it with a minimum amount and purchase some silver or gold first and then pay your bill, which will help you build a strong credit background without any weirdness. Also, the purchase from the vendors within this book will help you establish Money Comes to Money reality. Don't ever forget that every time you pay a bill (big or small). Buy a Silver Eagle (any year) for the stash or buy bullion (squared block of silver instead of coins for diversity in your stash).

In All Times, Take a Look

Especially in the hard times, it is best to always practice the three R's: review, refinance, and retirement.[28]

Review bills, statements, and subscriptions. See what you can pay or postpone from paying and look for a reduced payment.

Refinance or call creditors and ask for mortgage reduction. Call your creditors and ask what they can do for you. Many of them reduced payments for people in my city when it was the epicenter of the Franken Germ.

Retirement. Funds in bonds, focus funds in dire needs first, buy check, live within your means. If you are light on cash, check on all areas that have cash on hand. Some insurance policies allow for a person to cash it in for money to aid them.

Remember history when the market took a turn in 1929, 1971, 1978, 2001, and 2008, soon thereafter the market bounced back!

---

[28] Special thanks to Barbara Corcoran for this great advice on *Good Morning America.*

Bonus Love: God's Plan to Protect Folks[29]

A prudent man sees danger and takes refuge, but the simple keeps going and suffers for it.
—Proverbs 22:3

Times Square Church Emergency Preparedness Plan (Parts Added)

Parts are being added to instruct all churches and former members that the Bible shares many areas where on Earth people have put something extra to the side for bad or rainy days. Even Jesus recommends it through the parable of the ten virgins.

Many in our time laugh about putting something extra to the side. Others have scoffed at the messages our own local and state governments share with us to do. Sadly, people think that nothing can happen or the government won't declare martial law, which would keep everyone either under curfew or sequestered until it's over. Partially based on the nefarious blatant disregard to past warnings, a great number of society falls into Proverbs 22:3 and puts others in the category of the ten virgins. Although many claim to be the five virgins who had their oil while the others were not ready to meet

[29] God's Plan to Protect His People from the Coming Depression (1998). Parts are added in for your perusal and based on certain financial laws passed that I find alarming since much of these laws are not spoken of unless you are in the legal and financial fields where there are so many changes. It's not about evolving, but it's more like "Wow, this happened and they passed that?"

the bridegroom. Actually they were the five unprepared virgins. Yes, those who do not take strong advice to put something aside or prepare is not a bad thing, and it doesn't make you a hoarder, a laughing matter, or an outcast.

In fact, the people laughed at are the ones that will be okay in a major disaster, a major snowstorm that leaves no pathway into anywhere for provisions. This can happen or you can be one of those people who laughed at others only to starve to death. The Bible makes it clear from Genesis, with the story of Joseph, how God had his hand on that man's life to bless his family and many nations that are around today. A time is coming when those who took heed will be all right and those who didn't, well, you were warned time and time again.

Whatever your position in life is, the responsibility falls squarely in the hands that you were told but paid it no mind at all. These are the ones who get desperate. We all know a lot of desperate people in the time of crisis. Remember Hurricane Katrina and Hurricane Sandy? Both hurricanes proved that people, cities, and America as a whole is not ready for the storms that shall come, not in her present state!

If martial law will be declared, many people are going to panic, but for those who know the Lord will be able to survive, give answers, and help those in need. Choices will have to be made. *Really???* goes into some detail of how a society like this will be seriously in chaos beyond comprehension. So to not be in this problem, pray, brace yourself, and while everything is going on in the first twenty-four hours, get out of the big city to a safe place. But if you cannot get out of the city, just do these simple things so you will be all right going forward. For those who don't know Jesus, you just better repent first before asking or demanding for help from God. Because in a time like that, many will curse God and hunt those that have a stash that can tide them over. Bear in mind, the wise will move like the Romans, and bad boys and girls will move in silence.

Without further delay, here are some basic steps of preparation. It is imperative to pray and ask God for directions on three primary areas we would need to prepare for: shelter, family security, and food.

This is presented because economic fallout from computer issues may lead to bank closures, business failures, blackouts, lack of public transportation and other disruptions of service, stripped supermarket shelves, crippled emergency services, and widespread criminal activity. All these are recipe for chaos and overwhelming mental and physical breakdown.

Is there going to be a purge? Yes, it shall happen worldwide, but that time will not yet come as per Revelation chapters 2 and 3. The sad part is many people have experienced this shortfall of finances to get groceries and meds in Greece. It also happened in Germany post-World War II, and a few other countries as well. When both hurricanes Katrina and Sandy came through its targeted areas, it was casual chaos that had people in stores buying everything from water, crackers, bread, and cereal, and the shelves were naked in five supermarkets around me. Because many people like Rev. Wilkerson stated, "People keep only enough food stored on their shelves to last until their next visit to the supermarket. But major disruption in our country's food delivery systems would quickly deplete supermarkets' food supply." All of what you read will happen. It is not a matter of where; it's a point to have things in place *now*. As food prices continue to rise and the governments of the world continue to print currency at an alarming rate, families and some friends will come to others' houses to stay for a visit only to have to remain there until things return back to *full normalcy*. For people have yet been priced out of their homes, but the ones that would like to own a home will have difficulty in obtaining a house unless they had people who can spot them some funds or precious metal to secure such a purchase. Pay attention to the financial laws in different states as they change to accept gold and silver as medium of exchange for payment of taxes and other things. It's happening right before your eyes, and sadly, few people are sharing this info. My hat goes off to the wise governors and legislators that have saved their constituents' lives by adding constitutional precious metals for paying taxes and other necessities that concern the residences of those states. Thank you for seeing the future…

Thoughts on Preparation

Most Americans currently consume much more food than they need. Therefore, in preparing for hard times, we need to consider changing both the quantity and type of food we eat on a daily basis. Emergency food preparation should involve stocking up on long-term, shelf-stable, storable food. This is the reason why you need to prepare, and should have done so during the Obama and Bush years. Yes, we need to be mindful around those years when hurricanes Katrina and Sandy came forth. How many people in your entire community never had food or water stocked up to hunker down? How many people saw empty shelves of bread, crackers, water, even children's water, rice cakes, and a whole host of other areas depleted? Think about a snowstorm that paralyzed the entire city of New York and other cities where food is trucked into a town near you. And for those who do have land and farm, pay attention, city folks need you for some crazy reason that our government should cease purchasing certain foods that can and are grown in the USA. Politics and bureaucracy seemed to foul things up. Lives are at stake!

First of all, the *Silver Report* [30] spoke about a thing that happened when there was too much rain, which is not being discussed in the pulpits much because it affects economics. Now, I don't want to be the bearer of bad news, but a budget, money, and the lack of it are economic needs that must be placed into focus as to why many in the cities and rural areas will die from hunger and will be homeless. See, all these settings are going on in life now, and we must keep in mind that Matthew 24, Luke 21, and Mark 13 happen to back up all your

---

[30] Silver Report Uncut. 2019. "Food Shortage Warning for 2019: Millions of Areas Sit Unplanted May Lose Their Farm." YouTube.

disbelief. All you have to do is not to worry but know that once the one world government is in place, Jesus Christ comes back and then the new world order begins. The final days of mankind, the tribulation, begins! Yes, the Bible speaks on the one world government. We know the next scripture shows he comes, then afterward and only then, Satan's Adam. This is the thirteenth Imam or Mujamahadeed, the son of perdition, and the man of sin, which are all the names that you will ever hear or read in the description of this individual according to Revelation 13.

This guy rises up in Germany first, the fourth kingdom on earth or the Fourth Reich as it was shared to me. This is where the Bible gets juicy, and at the last two chapters of Revelation, if you're saved then we win and if you are not saved, then I urge for you to get saved quickly. No matter how much food, water, medical supplies, guns plus ammo, I implore for you to make sure that your prayer closet is in order first before you start spending, researching, and running around crazy unnecessarily. So when the time comes for you to get your stock on after getting your prayer on, just keep in mind that it's always good to eat the sample foods first before you place an order for supplies. Because there is a wide range of food-storage options available, including dehydrated meals (just add water), military style "meals ready-to-eat" (MRE), commercially packaged survival rations, and regular canned goods. (Our use of "canned" here includes all types of foods sterilized and vacuum-sealed in metal, plastic, paper, or any other kind of long-term packaging.) Each storage option has advantages, but the most economical way to secure long-term storable food is by stocking canned goods.

The canned goods storage plan outlined below is a brief suggestion of minimum quantities that people of moderate means could store in case of a crisis. In suggesting this list, we make the following assumptions:

- ✓ If used sparingly, the suggested items should last approximately sixty days.
- ✓ Regular store-bought meat, milk, and other perishables will not generally be available to consumers.

- ✓ Suggested items commonly sold in cans, bottles, or storable package form have a shelf life typically measured in months or, in some cases, years.
- ✓ People who require special diets should determine whether the levels of sodium, sugar, fat, or cholesterol in the suggested items might adversely affect their health.
- ✓ Careful attention should be paid to instructions concerning the reconstitution of dehydrated items with water.
- ✓ Choices may be made from all the suggested food groups based on personal taste and availability of items.
- ✓ Besides stocking the following suggested food items, people should have the following handy items: airtight bins with lids, battery-operated lamps, and hand-powered appliances.

Food Storage

The following list suggests storage necessities for one person. For two people, simply double the amounts, and for three or four people, triple the amounts. For larger numbers of people, use your discretion.

- ✓ Vegetables—twenty-four fifteen-ounce cans. For example: corn, carrots, potatoes, yams, greens, tomatoes, spinach, and green beans.
- ✓ Soups—twenty eight-ounce cans or dried.
- ✓ Hot cereal—six sixteen-ounce packages. For example: oatmeal, cream of wheat, cornmeal, grits.
- ✓ Cold cereal—three six-ounce packages. For example: granola, toasted oats, corn flakes, raisin bran.
- ✓ Beans and peas—twenty-four fifteen-ounce cans. For example: kidney, baked, green, and lima beans; sweet peas, split peas, lentils.
- ✓ Meat—fifteen sixteen-ounce cans. For example: sausages, Spam, chicken, ham,[31] corned beef, meatballs, and turkey.
- ✓ Meat alternatives—one two-pound package of dry egg powder and one twenty-four-ounce jar of peanut butter.
- ✓ Seafood—ten six-ounce cans. For example: tuna, sardines, herring, salmon.

---

[31] Many people who know me personally know well that I don't eat pork. But I will include it here for those who do and other items being reprinted for specific direction going forward in the years of reprieve while President Donald J. Trump was in office. Also, prepare for a famine coming shortly due to sources and recently confirmed talks. I will discuss this more in *Really???: The Amendment—One of Reasons of the Rapture Is Corruptible Seed.*

- ✓ Assorted fruit—twenty-four fifteen-ounce cans. For example: orange, apple, grape, fruit punch, and prune.
- ✓ Fruit blends and dried fruits—twenty sixteen-ounce cans. For example: fruit cocktail, cranberry sauce, and apple sauce. Also ten four-ounce packages of assorted dried fruits. For example: raisins, dates, and prunes.
- ✓ Milk—fifty ten-ounce packages of any long-lasting milk product, such as Parmalat or powdered milk.
- ✓ Pasta—ten one-pound packages of assorted pasta.
- ✓ Rice—one ten-pound bag or ten one-pound bags of minute rice.
- ✓ Crackers—five sixteen-ounce boxes of all kinds.
- ✓ Combination foods—five sixteen-ounce packages of tortillas, two large boxes of stuffing mix, and five one-pound packs of assorted seeds and nuts, such as sesame, sunflower, walnuts, peanuts, and pecans. (Snack foods may be stored with a shelf life of at least six months to a year.)

Also, stock any items you may anticipate needing from the following list: baking powder, baking soda, salad dressing, salt, sugar, oil, butter, mustard, mayonnaise, black pepper, cold beverage mix, cornstarch, wheat germ, jelly, meat extender, parmesan cheese, gelatin powder, jello, vinegar, lemon juice, powdered seasonings, butter powder, solid margarine, maple syrup, honey, coconut cream, bouillon cubes, nonstick cooking spray, paper products, pet supplies, butane lighter, waterproof matches, plastic film, aluminum, flashlight.

Also, make extra provisions for denture needs, eyewear, eye care, hearing aids, prosthetic and orthopedic devices, et cetera. And begin storing items now. Don't procrastinate.

Helpful Hints

Conservation

- ✓ Use stored items sparingly; extend their use for the duration of their shelf life.
- ✓ Practice now using less water for showers, washing, cooking, etc.
- ✓ Learn to use leftovers; do not discard unused but storable food.
- ✓ Plan all meals ahead of time in order to economize and avoid waste (like if you're in a blackout situation, then you may want to make all your preparations during the day for the night and set aside snacks for later).

Loss of Electricity

- ✓ A crisis may mean loss of cooking gas and home heating, so it's important to make contingency plans.
- ✓ Regular shopping for refrigerated and perishable items should continue until loss of electricity or food shortages forces you to revert to your emergency supply.
- ✓ Keep a supply of long-burning candles.
- ✓ If power goes out, many perishable food items can remain usable (at your discretion) for several days if your refrigerator is opened to a minimum.
- ✓ Frozen foods may still be eaten (at your discretion) if they're frozen in the center. Leave to finish defrosting.

- ✓ If there is snow outside or the outdoor temperature is no more than 40 °F (4.5 °C), some items may be discreetly "shelved" on a windowsill to maintain freshness.
- ✓ Use refrigerated and other perishable items first, including foods with the shortest shelf life.

Money

- ✓ Reduce your spending levels now and avoid incurring new debts of any kind.
- ✓ Set aside $10 to $20 per week at home in a safe place.
- ✓ It is vitally important to keep as much cash on hand as you can reasonably secure.

Storage Basics

- ✓ It is always better to use fresh produce (of verifiable quality), if it's available, and to keep canned or preserved goods on hand for less bountiful times.
- ✓ Many prepackaged and vacuum-sealed (canned) foods must be consumed within a short time after opening the container to avoid food poisoning.
- ✓ Consider storing canned foods under a bed or in a closet, if other storage space is not available.
- ✓ Keep canned foods away from direct sunlight.
- ✓ Never use a swollen or punctured can; it may cause botulism.
- ✓ Frequent opening of containers could cause items to spoil; keeping food in glass containers allows you to examine food contents without having to open them. You should clearly label all other storage containers.
- ✓ To prevent insect infestation in flour, cornmeal, sugar, rice, pasta, beans, cereals, etc., add a few bay leaves and store in airtight containers (for example, a plastic tub with a mylar liner) away from moisture.

Water

- ✓ Although we cannot be certain, experts do not expect water shortages to last more than thirty days.
- ✓ Plan to store enough water for drinking, cooking, and hygiene for one month—perhaps twenty-five gallons.
- ✓ Use water for personal hygiene sparingly (for example, three times per week).
- ✓ Prepare food in batches in order to save time, fuel, and water.
- ✓ Reduce washing of pots by making one-pot meals, such as stews, rich soups, stir-fry dishes, etc.
- ✓ Use disposable eating ware to save on dish and utensil washing.
- ✓ Baby wipes and antibacterial cleaners can reduce the need for water used in washing hands (but nothing feels better than washing hands in soap and water, amen).

Hygiene

- ✓ Store hygiene products in quantity, including soap, toothpaste, mouthwash, deodorant, tissue, feminine supplies, baby diapers, bed pan with plastic liner, lye, disinfectant, air freshener, chlorine bleach.

First Aid

- ✓ Fill two months' worth of prescriptions if possible.
- ✓ Buy an ample supply of vitamins and mineral supplements.
- ✓ Purchase first-aid items, including bandages, pain relievers, antacids, laxatives, antiseptics, etc.

Cooking

- ✓ Build main dishes around pasta or grains, with meals such as rice and beans.

- ✓ Stock up on canned heat, such as sterno.
- ✓ Budget your use of fuel wisely. Your fuel will have to last until supplies become available or normalcy returns.
- ✓ If possible, you may heat cans of food directly, but first remove the label, then puncture the top to let the steam out.
- ✓ Be sure the room is well ventilated to allow fumes to escape.
- ✓ When using a heat source, secure loose clothing and store flammable items in a safe place.

Baby Care

- ✓ Infants older than six months may be fed same food as the family, if it is pureed or ground in a blender and is prepared without additives. Exceptions are casseroles, pizza, cobblers, meat pies.
- ✓ Do not season baby foods; they should not have added sugar, salt, fat, MSG, etc.
- ✓ Do not use fried, greasy, brined (pickles, sauerkraut), processed (sausages), or high-calorie (candy, sodas, cakes) foods.
- ✓ Avoid using honey due to possible salmonella contamination.
- ✓ Fresh or canned juice is preferred over powdered or packaged beverages.
- ✓ Formula. Ready-to-eat: twelve eight-ounce cans. Concentrate: four eight-ounce cans. Powder: eight fifteen-ounce cans.

Suggested Sixty-Day Food Storage Plan for an Infant at Least One Year Old

- ✓ Iron-enriched baby cereal: two sixteen-ounce boxes of the following: rice, barley, wheat, or toasted oats.
- ✓ Vegetables: sixty six-ounce jars of any of the following: squash, sweet potato, or mixed vegetable.

- ✓ Fruit: sixty six-ounce jars of any of the following: pears, peaches, apples, plums, or strawberries.
- ✓ Meat and dairy: sixty six-ounce jars of any of the following: turkey and rice, beef, chicken or pasta; forty eight-ounce packages of any long-lasting milk product, such as Parmalat or powdered milk.

Now in this section are the added things that I suggest are valuable for the parallel reasons as stated by the late Rev. David Wilkerson and for discussions that I have had personally with rich, middle class, wealthy, poor, ballers, working poor. Wherever you are on North American soil, this and more items are suggested necessary to have. Some from various backgrounds have shared their opinion on what's going to happen, and others just think that everything is going to be all right if we print more money and pay people to stay home will hurt the supply side of the economy for all and it is imperative to review: because **HOLODOMOR 2.0** can manifest. Give your family a leg up in having a stash of food and other supplies before shelves go bare.

Items to Consider Based on the Laws

HR 4827 that was passed in Congress during the Obama administration. The following are listed for your perusal and for you to draw a clear understanding at what can and will happen in the future. However, under President Trump's administration, the Republican Congress passed HR 835 section 3 that backs our paper dollar with gold for now. Not a lot, but enough to make our money stronger according to the prophecy of *The Dollar Is Going to Judge the World* by Mark Taylor. It's happening now and will continue until after second plague has walked the land. So as it was discussed earlier, this is the section with reliable vendors that will accommodate all types of orders and ship to you discreetly by either UPS, FEDEX, and USPS. They deliver these items right to your door and send you an e-mail on when it's coming to you.

So you can prepare where to stack and stash items, I strongly recommend for you to get a safe. When bringing it into your house, apartment, or wherever you live at, bring a black oversized garbage bag and have the store clerk place the safe in the bag and then into the store bag. Most importantly, make sure that you are able to pick it up with ease. Now if you're going to store weapons in a safe, they make a special kind of safe for those items. I don't know the policies on that, so without further delay, let us begin.

Remember to check sodium levels in the MREs. Many of the foods that I suggested ship you a sample package that you can pay anywhere from $10 to $40 to try the food out during the good times so that you know what you have and how it taste. It makes no sense buying food and storing it away only to find out that the food tastes nasty or it's not what you exactly wanted in a time when you can't get anything else for a while. And most of all, think of your family, friends, and neighbors. Don't overextend yourself and make yourself a target for crime to occur. People are robbing people for food. There was a seven-seven-year-old lady who got hit in the head for her pizza. This is sad, and it's going to get worst. My parents shared that with me fourteen years ago before they passed, and WE ARE LIVING SOME OF IT OUT.

Vendors Suggested by Many of My Friends and Others I Have Dealt With

Augason: 800-878-0099
Legacy: 888-524-4185

Life Long Depot: Make sure that you order the crackers and deserts. Trust me, when it comes to snacks and you can't go to the store, this comes in handy. Also, there are no sample packs. Type into Amazon then check them out.

Nu Manna: 888-597-0775
Wise: 888-349-9124

My Patroit Supply: patroitsupply.com, 866-229-0927. They have seventy-two-hour sample packs. Invest in the food to see how it tastes, and should you like it, you can give them a call about other products.

Heirloom Seeds
Heaven's Harvest: heavesharvest.com, 800-516-4773

Precious Metals:[32] Their prices are on point, and I heard that their merchandise is vast for whatever you're looking for regarding coins, bullion, currency of the past, and a few other items. They offer a wide variety and ship discreetly to your door as well and offer prices based on the market, just like all gold and silver vendors; the only difference is that special offers are available when you ask them.

Little Coin Company: PO Box 5000, Littleton, NH 03561-5000; LittletonCoin.com; 800-645-3122. They offer a coin for your first order and when you fill in the relaxed price circular.

U.S. GOVMINT.com: 14101 Southcross Drive West, Suite 175, Burnsville, Minnesota 55337; 1800-456-2466.

U.S. Gold Bureau: 1908 Kramer Lane, Bldg. B, Ste. 300, Austin, Texas 78758; USGOLDBUREAU.COM; 800-775-3504.

National Collector's Mint, Inc.: 2975 Westchester Ave. Ste. 300, Purchase, NY 10577-2500, 1800-799-MINT; twenty-four hours a day, seven days a week.

Also, this bulletin below gives us a tip to keep close even when others do not believe you at all.

---

[32] My best advice is buy when the market is down. Get more for your order.

Silver Prices Going Back Up to $50 to $100 per Ounce?

Are silver prices poised to erupt again? Many experts are calling for another bull market in silver in the near future—one that could equal or even surpass the last one, when silver reached an all-time high of $50 per ounce. While we're not prognosticators, we do know that there are many factors that point to the potential for significant price movement.

Sharp increases in historical silver prices show an increase of almost 450% in the last fifteen years—an average increase of about 30% per year!

Bursts of activity in the silver market have caused silver prices to jump 50% last year alone!

Silver supplies have failed to keep pace with demand causing a shortfall of 147.5 million ounces last year!

According to the latest reports from the silver institute, global silver investment is 23% higher than the preceding ten-year average, totaling $4.4 billion!

Data in the latest World Silver Survey shows continued strong investment in silver bars and coins with purchases soaring 560% in the last fifteen years!

What happens when your money has the star at the end of the serial number?

They are on various different denominations of our paper currency. Also, it is okay to look through your money and see if you have any of these bills that have a star like the three you see above. These are more valuable than the face value of the denomination that it's replacing. It means that this is a substitute note. Sometimes you may have to go through all of the stash just to find the bills that meet the criteria for new monies hidden within your own stash. These soldiers will bring you back new and more money for the stash. The websites are www.answers.com and www.mycurrencycollection.com/reference/star.

Because you have enjoyed this moment of saving your money, I must include this tip:

To add a bit more fun into stashing. When you have three separate stashes going at the same time and to simplify the growth of three stashes, make sure your deposits are divisible by three; 15, 30, 45, 60, 75, and 90 can all be divided equally to feed all three stashes. This is your goal while taking whatever funds in your wallet the night before payday, and it goes into the investment/emergency stash. The fourth stash is mandatory to keep healthy, because the others can be replaced. Just add three times the monies you borrow from yourself and all shall be all right. If you just choose to borrow from yourself and don't replenish what you borrowed, all the work you did to accumulate your stash was a waste. The objective is always having wiggle room, and repaying yourself with extra is discipline and keeps one from being on low funds. Got it?

Now, for example, one lady on the train was reading my text messages while leaving Brooklyn crossing the bridge into Manhattan. I discussed with this woman the purpose of paying back three times the money you borrow from yourself. The other woman did not see the logic of paying three times the amount of funds back. This positions you to practically never need to borrow funds from anyone or depend on a plastic as option versus obligation and liability. It's time to live within your means and keep funds on hand for you to break the disease of depend-on-others-ism; besides, a person is worthy for the work of their hands.

Psst, guess what? This will make the banks mad! So under the first amendment and the fourteenth amendment, you are now armed with equal protection of the law to protect your best interest, your capital. Whether you worked hard or worked smart, capital is the one resource we all need before our paper money is no longer good. HR 4827 tells us the "Death of the Dollar" ordered by Congress and signed by former President Obama.

Oh, by the way, put things in order. Always keep a printed copy of your receipts from the bank; don't be like others who went through an evacuation and didn't have things in order.

My conclusion is that the entire book is designed to help you in a variety of ways. Have a stash, a plan, a person you trust, and most of all, accept Jesus as your Lord and Savior before the start of Gog and Magog War that will trigger the tribulation in the Book of Revelations from chapter 4 until 22. Also, continue to practice the 20% rule, a principle which keeps you in the plus side of life and makes you accountable for money.

Object of Sowing

The object of sowing brings about a result called reaping, which brings a manifestation that what you planted to the side will grow. You eat when you're hungry; well, your stash is hungry and needs more to grow. That's why when I got a secured credit card, my first purchase was 1 gram 24-karat bars. Then I paid it off and bought the max of the card in silver coins only to prep the stash. After all, money comes to money, and gold and silver command paper money to submit to you. The portion of funds set aside can help you walk or sit on a cushion.

Sowing and reaping is simply giving a smile and getting a smile back, even when wearing a mask. You hold the door for someone, and doors are held for you. Now *door* is singular and *doors* is plural. That means that it came back with interest. You know how to operate in the supernatural and natural tactic of sowing and reaping. You are blessed with a secret automatic double-portion blessing on everything they touch. Yes, even a door and the ones that have mastered this one component are never broke! Technically, many people know that sowing and reaping outdo karma and astrology. Ask yourself how many times you have given a person something then out of the blue someone gives you something you need as well. Sowing and reaping carries blessings with interest, twofold, sevenfold, tenfold, hundredfold, and pursuant to Mark 25:14–30 (talents, money), Genesis 1:26 (fruitful and multiple), and Proverbs 6:31 (thief is found and has to repay seven times), which breaks the spirit of idleness, a.k.a. boredom, along with evil thoughts. This is contrary to Jeremiah 29:11 (plan and longevity) and Psalm 122:7 (peace within thy borders). All these keep you blessed in the field and blessed in the city (Deuteronomy 28:4), whereas karma[33] doesn't have interest, gains, futures, shares, and generationally inherited built-in. It's solely based on action, while sowing and reaping is based on concurrent established principles that superimpose all things of prosperity to surrender to you.

Sample Debt List

	Problem's Name (Name of Debt)	Suggested Full Payment with Interest	More than Minimum Payment	Money Saved from Early Payoff	Priority Payment	Done Paying/ Stash Time	Months in Bondage
1.							
2.							
3.							
4.							
5.							
6.							
7.							
8.							
9.							
10.							
11.							
12.							
13.							
14.							

[33] According to *Merriam-Webster*, karma is a force generated by a person's actions held in Hinduism and Buddhism to perpetuate transmigration and, in its ethical consequences, to determine the nature of the person's next existence.

Sample Debt List

	Problem's Name (Name of Debt)	Massaging the Bondage with Interest	More than Minimum Payment	Money Saved from Early Payoff	Priority Payment	Done	Months in Bondage
1.							
2.							
3.							
4.							
5.							
6.							
7.							
8.							
9.							
10.							
11.							
12.							
13.							
14.							

Stack and Stash List Page

	Personal Stash	Stack and Stash Pile #1	Stack and Stash Pile #2	Stack and Stash Pile #3	Investment/ Emergency Stash	Silver and Gold, Other Financial Tools	Total Stash on Hand
1.							
2.							
3.							
4.							
5.							
6.							
7.							
8.							
9.							
10.							
11.							
12.							
13.							
14.							

Stack and Stash List Page

	Personal Stash	Stack and Stash Pile #1	Stack and Stash Pile #2	Stack and Stash Pile #3	Investment/ Emergency Stash	Silver and Gold, Other Financial Tools	Total Stash on Hand
1.							
2.							
3.							
4.							
5.							
6.							
7.							
8.							
9.							
10.							
11.							
12.							
13.							
14.							

Stack and Stash List Page

	Personal Stash	Stack and Stash Pile #1	Stack and Stash Pile #2	Stack and Stash Pile #3	Investment/ Emergency Stash	Silver and Gold, Other Financial Tools	Total Stash on Hand
1.							
2.							
3.							
4.							
5.							
6.							
7.							
8.							
9.							
10.							
11.							
12.							
13.							
14.							

Personal Notes

Personal Notes

Personal Notes

Critical Update: Franken Germ Alert!

The last-minute amending I would like to make for all the readers and all the people we love is that we must remember that this is not to create panic. I want you to have a heads-up before anything transpires going forward. Remember, this is totally out of love and care for you and the family. Before making heavy decisions, pray first and stand on the Word.

There is a great deception that was done to both our president and the world, putting all people in danger on earth. I was watching some television one day when the NYC Transit told the media[34] that they clean and disinfect the trains every seventy-two hours. Then on March 11 to 12, they changed policy within forty-eight hours to twice a day. Look, without the medical martial law, which is the pandemic, the NYC Transit never would have changed positions on cleaning all the trains and buses. Why did they change face in their cleaning of the subway? In one news conference their representatives were extremely vocal and animated about whatever it is that caused them to clean more, which means one thing: they know something more than they can share publicly. Like I stated earlier, I care for you, the reader, so as new developments approach my desk, you will know![35] Have a great and God-blessed day. Pray, because our lives depend on it every day.

---

[34] All channels, including WABC-TV channel 7, Fox Five News channel 5, and all the others during their press conference on March 11–12, 2020.

[35] Follow me on Twitter @Jabbarthewatch1 and you will be shocked at the info that comes your way.

In a special report on WABC–TV channel 7, I listened to the governor of New York State who seemed clueless as to why people came to the hospital sick and died some forty-one days later in some cases and others died in droves. Also, this write-up comes because COVID-19 is more like Franken Germ that has a mission to steal, kill, and destroy—sounds like the devil—but wants to seal the deal that you leave this earth before your time. Where did it come from, and why? It was answered that it came from the cleptocratic clown pukes (CCP) that allegedly released what they thought was the safe version on the crowd. It was the lethal strain which caused the problem. Seeing that this was a problem, the safe strain was released and then people started traveling from Wuhan, China, all over the world. That is where it gets weird. Among the first cases that hit the USA, one man came to the hospital and looked horrible. This was outside of Seattle, Washington. And then twenty-four hours later, the man felt better and walked out of the hospital like new money. There were other cases of people being sick and coming in with an unknown pneumonia, and within a week or three, they were dead. The nurses faced that. Sadly, the Black and Brown people are not the highest amount of people dead since both cultures only make up about 37% to 39%, or 43% of the entire North America populace. So in truth, statistically, the bulk of the people who died was Caucasian, Asian, Persian, and others on this soil. There is wrong information running. What made transit take this entire matter of contagion so seriously? Why is there a ban in riding the subways for essential workers? Was it the fact that a man collapsed on a train and stopped moving only to expose others to the Franken Germ? Was it the fact that an official's request for two million body bags sparked alarm from elected officials? Was this plague so dangerous that we needed the National Guard? That's just the start of some things. Was the intention of the plague all about for us to see fear, destruction of our economy, and stoppage of our livelihood? Others warned us some fifteen years ago, and there is blood on the hands of those who knew, which is totally wrong.

And So It Begins . . . Man Drops Dead on NYC Subway - Coronavirus

Those people who were doing the warning and were in Congress from the 1990s to present, knew what was in the federal stockpile. But they failed us, and that's why we should not put our trust in mankind, but in God. For the Lord is my strength in the times that don't seem too good, and he should be yours too.

When a privy information was relayed to me, I was shocked to learn some things. It is not a conspiracy theory, and yes, we should all wear gloves, mask, earplugs, and eye protection while traveling on the subway system in New York City. Not just because others are doing it. Some loose brain may state, "He's being xenophobic or racist." It's a choice that we should make, like the health care workers who don't want to expose their loved ones or others in their travels. It's not the germs, dirt, and other things that are disturbing, it's the combination of the fact that raises questions: Was it due to a man dying on the train before this outbreak? Did it take the first wave of the outbreak to self-quarantine the problem? It was more than that. This was being contagious and zoonotic. It was quietly shared in confidentiality, and many people never saw or noticed the changes in protocol. It was the political wording "If you don't feel well, just stay home." Just keep in mind this is out of love and to let you know that our government has been lied to! Remember, they have been lied to so badly that they are slow walking their findings to the public to prevent any enemies from getting the glory of how many people died by this bioweapon. Also, Iran, Italy, South Korea, Japan, and Russia have all not kept accurate numbers because all countries want to keep their land, people, and prosperity uninterrupted. The Wuhan Health Oppressors (WHO) is detrimental to *all* human rights on earth, and because their funding depends on the narrative, they modify it for the world. This makes them too unreliable and controllable yet easy to allow them to speak to the world while China's Xi Jinping tries to put the fire out only to want global domination.

The first thing that we need to speak about is the fact that a communist country has lied, along with the Wuhan Health Oppressors

(WHO) which has not been working in our best interest. For such matters, going forward, I will make my point standing on Ezekiel 33:3 and bless you with a heads-up pursuant to Genesis 12:3, "I will bless those that bless you and curse those that curse you." They could have told the truth because it was slow walked to them, but they lied numerous times to all of us on TV with live coverage. The other reason that this was needed to be in your hands is because the city of New York has changed position on not wearing face mask to wearing a face mask. There were also campaigns to wash hands, and many of us have gloves to wear outside and soap used for washing hands. But honestly, I truly feel that someone came to my city and set something off in the New Rochelle, Westchester, first allowing a level of martial law to occur. Since updates are common once a pandemic has been announced, this places our nation into a medical marital law presently with a likelihood that there is going to be lockdowns due to the possible fact.

The Six Weeks of Pain

After President Trump closed the US borders in January 2020, despite objections to keep it open, my city and state—New York—didn't initiate lockdowns in full until March 15, 2020 *strongly*!

Now state-health officials issued an update on March 17, which the worldwide *count* was "183,350" cases, 7,176 deaths, and 69,142 (reported by *WION News*) recovered people, yet we still don't see how many people tested don't have this dreaded bioweapon in their system. In this final update, it proves our president was lied to when on Gravitas "Wuhan Virus pandemic" leaked audio, featuring WHO officials reveal China's lapses is in a seven-minute video and on time stamps 5:53 to 5:26, and also here, a second time 4:44 to 4:14 literally states, "It's absolutely important at this point. And not so that we have all the data as an organization, so we can *protect China*." This very statement appears to end that portion of the recording on YouTube wasn't erased or deleted. It's like everyone now feels like we can share the truth because no one is going to do anything to me… After January 2020, the WHO kept praising China's response publicly while these deceptive practices seem good until it hits home. The worst is yet to come!

Now at this point, sources of three decades ago shared the facts about a lot of people going to hospitals, nursing homes, the exact culture who is mostly dying the most (fluctuates, depending on the *state you live in*); being that about two million people may have died within my city, and it explains in between the lines how spooked the governor and mayor are to fully reopening after shutting almost everything *down*. That the body count was not made public officially until March, which means that many people who went to the hospitals during this period were not counted or included in the body count, and for all reasons going forward, the likelihood that the extended lockdowns is because this is more than AMBERS, it can be the start of the third wave. Because New York State, New Jersey, Connecticut had their second wave during May/June period of this year, with children having outbreaks equal to that of being bitten by an African black mamba, which prompted the governor of New York State to look really spooked. And further talks from other people within those buildings and the area stated *"when a person went out by ambulance from a luxury apartment,"* the building would later *become close to vacant really quickly*, and many my sources have shared *much info that would shock you!* But the facts are the truth, we have not seen anything yet, and many fellow New Yorkers believe that this is just the beginning of something really serious and ugly to come, which shall require prayer. Also, I totally believe that a heavy wave of death has come forth because of not enough equipment for nurses, too many dead, and not enough places to put them, and the fact that China has been selling slum equipment to America and other places in the world for their own gain is our pain. The price manipulation and defective medical supplies are a problem that shows the world that China cannot be trusted.

A Real Slum Move

I believe that a heavy buy on all masks was done ahead of time; my opinion then is the same now, confirmed that 730 million face masks and other PPE masks, respirators, public and health-care supplies was all procured by China and then faulty equipment was sold to all the world. God don't like ugly, and this wrong will cost them dearly. The consumers of 122 countries have stopped buying anything made in China. I read the article, and it basically links them to the plague of death that has killed millions and infected eight tigers and lions (zoo), two housecats (New York State), and one dog, and human-to-animal transmission makes this a plague. Misinformation is sad, and this is not a virus!

We don't need the government of another country to lie continuously just to save face. Secondly, WE, THE PEOPLE of this great nation, need to be on point despite what another government wants to lie to our president and the world about this highly contagious zoonotic Franken Germ. You probably are wondering why I call it Franken Germ. When I call this wildly combined additives that make this a cocktail component of enhanced mutation of being the perfect biological weapon of our time, I am not praising the makers of this abomination of demonic boredom. Nope! It's deeper than that. Because I do know whatever one person reaps, he shall sow. That applies in good, and it has interest when it's bad. So I hope that they understand that whatever plans they have *shall not work.* And because there was a release of this foulness China thinks that they will have a war with the USA, but they are wrong. They look forward to such, but it will not happen. There shall be two countries that will fight, gain ground, invade, and capture the truth of what happened with the release of the Franken Germ twins. There will come a surprise that China will get, and the entire world will see it happen and be shocked because whatsoever you do in the darkness shall come to light. Also, all the people responsible in aiding the kleptocratic clown posse within the United States federal government shall see justice even for their roles in all levels of thievery, both seen and unseen shall be dealt with, and the media will not be able to hide.

The Franken Germ Twins

Its name is based on the theory of roach baits. It goes attached on the carrier until they shed some of the poison where the healthy are at and attacks the nest right there. This is slightly different. It attacks people causing pain and death fast in its design; plus to cause fear, panic, and havoc on the global markets. We all have been overwhelmed with hearing about the COVID-19, and many people are not happy about this zoonotic contagion. This had many nervous, and others avoid hearing the newscasters discuss the topic of which has majority of NYC under quarantine for a lengthy time. But the problem is, there needs to be a cure that can help patients entering hospitals in both NYC and other state or city hospitals too. Has anybody wondered what and why so many people became extremely sick, resulting in overcrowding and possibly with no real test that works for our nation? How do we deal with a sickness that has no symptoms yet causes the body's vital organs to quit? It is this problem that has gripped the world and killed plenty in the line of duty: friends, family, first responders, and most importantly those in Hong Kong protest last year at the start of the outbreak.

I'm not taking sides. But China did issue a state of emergency in November 2019 during the Hong Kong protesting, and a shady impeachment trial without the witness commenced. One Russian family heard and saw the declared state of emergency and asked for their children to come home; they declined and hunkered down. Nevertheless, the Hong Kong protestors were greeted with tear gas. Many didn't get up quickly, while others collapsed or needed help from the protest zone. The Chinese New Year commenced and then the spread began with many dying from symptoms that were yet fully publicized, except for the *wash-your-hands campaign.* Yet the thing that is slow-walked and overlooked is that the Novel Coronavirus, a.k.a. COVID-19 with its medical name SARS-CoV-2, has made its mark. But what hit the USA is called Nipah. This is not coronavirus. It is the Nipah virus. It comes from fruit bats, where the cycles of much more virulent strains of the Nipah virus are found.[36] The WHO knew about this in August 2018. This is a zoonotic contagious plague that came out in 2018 and killed a lot of people according to the Wuhan Health Oppressors (WHO) which hid the truth about this Franken Germ. They have seen this before and didn't want to call it a pandemic because they were scared. Gee, American money of $400 million per year must have made their organization blind! Newscasters discussing the topic of whom or how many are in quarantine in hospitals is spooky, but they barely report negative results, which is strange and detracts from giving hope to people who are not infected and sitting in isolation under this medical martial law.

A gospel show spoke on it and one other confirmed the information that there is a new sickness and two strains of it on US soil. These two[37] distinct versions of the Franken Germ are named L-strain and S-strain. The L-strain is more aggressive and faster spreading than S. The S-strain is the safe version. Alarmingly 70% of patients and those cremated have caught the aggressive L-strain. These two strains get people sick, and once sick from one, you are not immune from the other. That's where it gets weird, because its baseline's contents and it is grossly combined with the results of what other scientists have scoffed at. The findings are serious enough to raise an eyebrow or two.

Its contains a bilateral baseline of both Middle Eastern Respiratory Syndrome (MERS) and Severe Acute Respiratory Syndrome (SARS). NYU School of Medicine Professor Philip Tierno Jr. stated, "It was possible that the disease was biphasic, meaning symptoms could go away before returning again later on. Once you have infection, it could remain dormant and with minimal symp-

---

[36] Do Prophecies Say Virus Hits USA? Stan at Prophecy Club dated February 27, 2020.

[37] Two Strains of Coronavirus! March 4, 2020.

toms, and then you can get an acceleration if it finds its way into the lungs."

Phase 1 causes fever, cough, congestion in the lungs, and myigea (muscle twitches and pain). Then it seems to go away, but it doesn't. People have been released from hospitals showing no trace of the active virus, then suddenly drop dead on the streets from heart failure.

Phase 2 attacks the vital organs, kidneys mostly, feeling achy and tired. Thinking it will pass, they go on with their daily life. But actually inside them the Franken Germ has sent them into sepsis. They drop dead from septic shock and organ failure. The government is not telling you this because they don't want you to panic. But the WHO lied[38] to the entire world.

One version of anthrax has the ability to kill 130,000 to 3,000,000 per a certain amount. This COVID-19 does behave exactly like all that are mentioned above, and according to the issues one would have, it's ten times worse than the flu. As a virus, it would need the help from a host, where viruses are able to multiply. That's good for the virus, but not good for the host. This is how the L-strain infect aggressively and then the S-strain was to reverse the effects of the lethal strain and allow them to be okay as if nothing had happened.

Yet the final two ingredients make it fast-acting and allows it to mutate quickly. It is HIV that mutates into one or six different strains of AIDS naturally and elements of malaria, yet the mutation infects like it has the behavior of anthrax added. According to Italy and French scientists, when patients die, they die of this plague. They die from a variety of damage to vital organs that makes this a viral pathogen such as those who died of pneumonia with Acute Respiratory Disease Syndrome. This makes the lungs wet and heavy, and this causes inflammation and infection. Is it just the sequence of HIV? Why were the patients who died found to have Chlamydia

---

[38] Hal Turner. 2020. "COVID-19: What You're Not Being Told by Officials or Media: This will Be Survival of the Fittest. The Rest will Die." HalTurnerRadioShow.com.

pneumonia? How was this not found, and what is really going on? If you test positive for Franken Germ, can you be accepted into the military? Public service?

No, one cannot enter the military after having the Franken–Germ from what was shared with me last year. Looking at some examples of asymptomatic transmissions.

According to officials from North Korea, the science of this Franken Germ is so contagious, it is spread by air, based on the following examples and some that will not be mentioned on television (maybe in part). An infected person can be coughing, sneezing, urinating, with bowel movements. The fact is that this same virus can live on nonporous surfaces for up to twenty-eight days, including door handles, public toilets, cashier counters in stores and supermarkets, computer keyboards, and mostly everything else. It flows through public sewer lines from toilet flushes, and then can evaporate up out of manhole covers. The virus has an 83% infection rate. That means if one hundred people get exposed to it, eighty-three of them will get sick. So if an infected person goes into a store or supermarket or public bathroom, a school, office, warehouse, or anywhere and touches products on shelves or coughs, the virus gets on the products in that store or supermarket, bathroom, school, office, warehouse, etc., and it can survive.

Then when you walk in a couple minutes, hours, or even days later and pick up the same item or even smell their stink in the bathroom, *pow*, you're infected. And that is not good at all.

Worse,[39] this virus can infect others through the eyes and ears. Let's say you're walking inside somewhere and an infected person was there minutes earlier and coughed or sneezed. The cough or sneeze threw microscopic entity in possession of the virus. Another thing that needs to be mentioned is a prime factor that a person can infect

---

[39] Proof: The novel coronavirus infecting the world is a military bioweapon developed by China's army (February 1, 2020). In 2005 China's defense minister speech "Bioweapon will Clean up America for China Invasion." (Here are some excerpts to prove that the Chinese openly discussed using biological warfare not only against the US, but on their own people. Their vast land is there to serve our need for mass colonization.)

others, about six people, without symptoms and will start showing later on because it's asymmetric. The reason why the first reporters of this Franken Germ stated that it is asymmetrical follows below:

In one apartment building in Hong Kong, a sewer vent pipe in a wall had a crack in it. The germ went up that vent pipe, got out a crack, and infected people in apartments several floors away from an infected family. We have to take it seriously and possibly look at other nations for resurgence after all the death stops or slows down.

Now can it be transferred to money?

Britain officials have warned their citizens to use alcohol sanitizer after handling money amid fears that the deadly coronavirus can be passed on via coins and banknotes. And to add insult to misery, the *Globe*, in an article titled "Virus Horror: Your Cash Could Kill You," sounded like the initiation of the American cashless society. Maybe not just yet? China has destroyed some four billion of bank notes which equaled to twelve tons in Wuhan and they are not out of the woods.

I use gloves when dealing with money, and if I really want to be extra, I put all the cash in a bucket of hot water with a cap full of Clorox and two caps of Breath of Pine. I include some prayer and then swish the money around in the water. Then I use a strainer and dry the money, stack it up, and stash it. Simple. This is not the time to go fully plastic as others think it's cool to do, but there may come a time when plastic will cease! And you will need to have cash!

There was a study of genes in 103 samples of the Franken Germ,[40] with its original name is SARS-CoV-2, Novel Coronavirus, and now COVID-19. It has brought forth a discovery of two distinct versions of it, named L and S. The L-strain is more aggressive. The

---

[40] www.halturnerRadio.com. April 2, 2020. The Coronavirus has mutated into at least two separate strains since the outbreak in December, according to Chinese scientists. Researchers say there are not two types of the same coronavirus infecting people, and most people seem to have caught the most aggressive from of it. According to "Two Strains of Coronavirus" (March 4, 2020) and "Engineered Novel Coronavirus Okay for Europeans" by Benjamin Fulford (January 29, 2020), a test was done in NYC and we got hit with the European strain of the Wuhan, China virus and also the Hanta virus (third one).

S-strain when combined with the L strain has attenuated the behaviors of the two combined to be parallel to a common cold. Sadly, I believe that this could have been far worse than what we are dealing with. Sadly, an alarming 70% of patients who died were cremated, yet a few autopsies caught the aggressive L-strain. These two strains get people sick, and once sick from one, you are not immune from the other. However, it was shared that China released the L-strain on people to try and save their own people, later on releasing the S-strain. That's why these combined strains if separate would have killed more people. (The L-strain which is lethal would have mutated every 340 infections, and the S-strain, which is safe, may have done nothing to reverse the process.) Yet in all, the numbers of dead are messed up, and it's unbeknownst to the USA that two strains are here plus one more. Those who died was hit with the lethal strain, and yes, they leaked both strains on purpose as a desperate attempt to stay in power. Xi Jinping is having instability within the ranks, and soon it's coming out! It will spill out and affect the market on their side causing investors to run! The fact of a nonchalant approach rejecting aid, monitoring, donations or assistance from the Wuhan Health Oppressors and the United States, but China wanted to keep the epidemic in a black box.

Getting coronavirus S-strain will give you immunity from when they released the L-strain that was to be released to carry out the colonization agenda of helping bring in the new world order. An agenda that is denied by the Blood of Jesus against all nefarious plans of this senseless murdering of innocent people. Stop their plans and dispatch 144,000 times 5 angels to stop this in Jesus's name. Amen and amen.

Looking back at history, the last plague that came forth lasted for three years, and I believe that this plague is going to be around for two years. China's Cleptocratic Clown Posse plan to release both this one and the other one because they're trying to make a big statement that will put the world on notice. But seriously, they have been doing too much. When one has been caught in a lie, they need to just chillax, but no, they want to prepare for war with India, Taiwan, Philippines, Viet Nam, Australia, and a few other nations including the USA. So before they want to start a war with one or all of those countries, don't they think it is time to *MAKE A DUAL CURE*?

The American government should make two cures, one for anthrax and the other using the antibodies with a combined mixture linked with vitamin D, iron, and Zinc to get rid of the Nipah. How do we know that this is Nipah? Let's discuss the effects on both male and female alike and why men in certain countries die in higher capacity and women die in lower capacity. Then it flips, and now it's attacking the children on North American soil, which is the resurgence. Plus, the protest that may trigger a new lockdown; I pray not. This is a weapon designed to prevent people from having children, and if any people in the future may have some unforeseen issues, I pray that you get all types of health assistance or be healed from this plague. Sadly, this is truly a bioweapon that has transformed into a plague. With the first human-to-animal infection, remember the tiger in the Bronx. Well, there were eight tigers and lions, two housecats, and one dog all infected in different parts of New York State and City. If you're a pet owner, get your family member checked out. That may not be the only case, and truthfully looking at this entire invisible problem we share on this soil, I humbly and sincerely pray that this is not the case with this Franken Germ.

The thing that really grips me is how it kills men in certain countries at higher rates and vice versa. The true reason why it targets certain people and nationalities, as originally reported, leaves all of us with a big concern for which it is imperative for men's health.

For Men's Health

From the research paper [41]

"The potential pathogenicity of the Franken Germ to testicular tissues, clinicians should pay attention to the risk of testicular lesions in patients during hospitalization and later clinical follow-up especially the assessment and appropriate intervention in young patients' fertility." This abomination has the ability to be a population-control weapon. The only thing that I know about this plague and how it affects women is oddly equivalent to the flu and then it starts to beat you up really fast.

My state actually went on YouTube to issue a one-minute gag order to police and EMS about who has the virus that you may have to engage with. Now from discussions with members of the health-care field, both retired and on active duty, all stated the same thing:[42] "Amongst all the people who come into emergency are not people who possess the one genetic marker called melancholy and we are not fully immune to this Franken Germ." Many of us who do not

---

[41] "Bulletin: Testicular Cells Are the Potential Targets of 2019 nCoV." February 15, 2020.

[42] Attention, Black and Brown folks, the media has forgotten us. During 9/11 it didn't happen to all the people who have the genetic marker of melancholy in their DNA. We can contract Franken Germ and we can beat it too by eating right, going to our doctors regularly for checkups, and eating healthier than before with vitamins C, D, Iron, and Zinc. A lot of us have bad eating habits, and those need to change, or it can cause us some problems in the future. For the Black and Brown folks, eat healthier without greasy content and so many sweets. If we don't look out for our health, can we depend on society to do the job? No, so every time you eat dinner, go for a walk for twenty minutes and then relax thereafter. It will work, and that's the change of improved circulation after eating instead of sleeping.

get it are blessed to have mild symptoms and no preexisting health conditions. For those who do get it and feel like they are on their way out of here, pray because many have rejected Jesus Christ's love. He can save you when the meds don't. Many people who survived this plague have a testimony to share and things in their lives that need to be finished or currently wrapping up. And for others, it was not their time to leave this earth and the people who love them. We love you all and wish for a speedy and full recovery in Jesus's name, Amen!

The Franken Germ was originally designed not to harm European descendants, but it has H1N1 genomes that make it contagious to infect the vulnerable ones (sixty years old and up) with existing medical conditions such as diabetes. And because there are two strains, it requires double work in making a cure that conquers the anthrax behavior part, and a cure for the AIDS/HIV portion would reverse the spread and help countless people in North America. That cure would have to be iron- and zinc-based to be one of the arsenal of adequate medicines to treat people in case they can't get the serum that kills Franken Germ. Before we get deeply into more factors, please be prepared for the next release of noxiousness; it's called the knockout blow in September to November. Position yourself for the next CCP attack on its people, which will affect a lot of us. We should know that another round of lockdowns is coming. Many of you were told to prepare but are still unprepared. Some are not paying attention to televised discussions that affect you and your household. We all learned a few things about previously elected people. We would have things in the stash, if wasn't for the previous four administrations. Especially those people who are still in Congress since last century should have been on their job truthfully. Then came former presidents George H.W. Bush (deceased), Bill Clinton, George W. Bush, and Barrack Obama and all their administrations. This is reasonably asserted because the Federal national stockpile was created in 1999. Who the president was and who were in Congress then were the ones who need to be held accountable and even those who are there prior and during the current president. What were they doing in office? Why were there no supplies?

When this bioweapon was created, it was to target a specific race, and a biracial counterpart is what I gathered from the first sources of information. Also, it is made to be contagious to anyone else that comes in contact with the infected and cocktailing it to enhance the mutation. This makes this one ugly bioweapon with properties that the regular coronavirus does not possess. What happens when this is over? Can a person test positive for malaria or HIV some five years later?

This germ is not normal and is not Novel Coronavirus, a.k.a. COVID-19! The reason why it's not COVID-19 is because China had ordered all pets killed. And in Mexico this poor man waited far too long until the disease became hemorrhagic ends. Yuck! This is the same plague that killed people in China, Japan, city of Qom in Iran, city of Milan in Italy; Spain, South Korea, Russia, Canada, but China collected and killed all pets because this is not COVID-19. This very germ was made in a laboratory and was designed to be asymptomatic. The quarantine should have been twenty-four days instead of fourteen. This is far from COVID-19. Heck no! This is definitely Nipah, and the sad part is that a second wave comes in May or June in most countries, but the knockout blow is September or November. A society, already on its knees, needs to remember the Word of God: "I bless those who bless thee, and curse those who curse thee" (Genesis 12:3).

The Nipah virus is communicable and that's why China killed all the pets and both China and Japan shut off the water system to add the deathblow to this Franken Germ. It comes from fruit bats, and the germ is zoonotic and very contagious. What makes it spread with a two-piece behavior? What makes this bioweapon designed to knockoff a certain race of people and endanger others through infection and put at risk other people that have ailments too? Since November 2019 there has been a widespread effect of this advanced germ which is equipped with HIV and has a two-stage behavior like anthrax. Like the theory of combat roach baits, this Franken Germ is a weapon that moves in fast, hurts people, and is designed to cause fear, panic, pain for markets, and to strangle any aspects of productivity. No, it was not designed by the USA, but we are all living a nightmare that makes any Congress folks stop taking swipes at each other and hopefully get things done without being childish. No, I won't name names today, but the problem the public sees is, like the shutdown of the government and the control of opening the economy, it was the choice of one person. As long as you remember, any speaker of the house has the *full control* of USA's wallet.

Now, the problem is that newscasters are scared, along with many on Capitol Hill. The news earlier today at ten in the evening on Fox TV, April 5, 2020, was discussing the areas of graves, crematories, and many other places which are overworked as they tend to the dead, thus finishing the entire report with a shot at the refrigerated trucks outside of Bellevue and Brooklyn Hospitals. This reminded me about a document in the UK, showing that the UK government is making plans for mass graves! And China recently bought and deployed forty portable furnace which can cremate fifty people per day. Multiply this by forty furnaces and that equals to two thousand bodies per day! There were some very strong inconsistent statements that went public especially when the eye in the sky showed a lot more. (See the questions later on and ask around for yourself.)

Have no fear,

DON'T OUR LIVES COUNT!!

The news shared with us came from WHO and the CCP. Many more of us know that America had its hand in COVID madness, yet we all have to search a matter out and keep our family safe. Combined with the power of faith in God and prayer, it is always going to work out great! Keep in mind that God goes before us, and he got our back because he is always by our side. Still pray that you put your key in the door of your house every day.

The zoonotic Franken Germ, a.k.a. COVID-19, is running through different countries, so let us all eat right, take vitamins, and make sure that you pray, because according to the Japanese, they are seeing that this virus is traveling through the old rusty pipes in one town. Yes, the very pipes they use for washing hands, showering, washing dishes, and more. This is mentioned because the news did not know about the details that both Japan and China knew; yes, they did cut off water supply because it was contaminated, which included the sewer system as well. This is not what's being shared to the general public, and it shows how contagious Franken Germ which can adapt to different environments too easily.

It has been shared to the public that this plague has been killing far more men than women. In some countries the pattern switches to more women than men. The gendered death gap was also seen in the smaller SARS and MERS outbreaks, according to Angela Rasmussen, a virologist at Columbia University. It is further stated that men in Italy made up 60% of people with confirmed cases of the virus and more than 70% of those who have died from Franken Germ, according to the country's main public health research agency. And in South Korea, 61% confirmed infections have been in women. This shows that this is a bioweapon. I will share my thoughts and belief that this bacterium is actually a military bioweapon that escaped lab custody with help; now it's become a plague which infected a tiger in the Bronx. How many other animals and pets are infected that we don't know about? Whether it was mishandled accidentally or intentionally released, *the truth will come out! Don't be surprised.*

The world death rate is at more than 21, 500,000 because of Franken Germ, and it is highly covered up by China to a certain degree. Iran, South Korea, North Korea, Italy (hardest hit in Europe), the United Kingdom of Great Britain, Russia, and sadly North America share in the grief of those people or group responsible for this demonic release of death on the earth. The cover-up is in the data from the cellular networks and the images of the open-aired cremation. The butt kicker is the amount of urns given back to the people of China. They cannot get rid of this proof and the fact that a civil war is about to kick off, making the entire production process in China going from bad to extremely worst. Also, there are food riots and all types of things going on over there. The breaking point will come and it will be disastrous for China to continue with a nonchalant attitude and will be paying the whole world reparations for sixty years. It will happen, and their economy is going to put a new meaning to "America's Great Depression of 1929" due to their negligence. Also, one culprit I feel gave a gross misdiagnosis between coronavirus and Nipah virus. It's a problem with trusting the WHO. China may have to close its borders causing Hong Kong to be economically destroyed. The Franken Germ is global and has no cure except the S-strain which may reverse the effects of this problem. But by now, their "cure" will not work, because after 340 people are infected, *it mutates*! No wonder the CDC has been super nervous about this Franken Germ. It is overly contagious and has the behavior of anthrax coupled with enhanced mutation of HIV and malaria. This makes this a lethal germ and too contagious! Its time is soon to be up. Watch and see.

The End

Last love note, there is a six-day treatment that came from a hidden peer review paper, and it's for six days to heal and better health. *If* infected by the Franken Germ for six days, one will need vitamins C, D, and zinc, which provide relief, combined with fluids and alkaline-based water. This study came out of Cleveland showed that people diagnosed with COVID-18 (Pakistan), 19 (worldwide), variant equals COVID-21. I heard a video that shared the cure is deadlier than the disease itself. This means to me that whatever you feel comfortable with, induce plenty of fluids, vitamins D, C, zinc. It provides relief in just six days or faster based on a study that was curtailed until now…not why would some sick Bum conspire to withhold this info, which would have mitigated our current problem.

One more thing, if one gets COVID-19 under New York State Case Law that in two cases brought to save their family members and kept two families from teary moments through their decisions supporting life, liberty, and the pursuit of the family's happiness—IVERMECTIN works! Thank you, justices of the New York Supreme Courts.

Questions

1) If there are only a few more than a thousand patients, why is it in Wuhan, a mega-city that hosts a number of nationally renowned mega-hospitals, people are working round-the-clock to build two makeshift hospitals in suburban Wuhan?
2) Can an agency that is funded by the world be honest and trustworthy on anything they say? Why didn't the WHO agency inform the world that this Franken Germ, a.k.a. COVID-19, is a zoonotic germ?
3. Since WHO knew about this, according to their website, didn't they compare notes from their files about the zoonotic outbreak in August 2018?
4. Is there much difference in the symptoms of Nipah virus and COVID-19 since both end in fatal encephalitis?
5. When are we going to take tighter measures and quarantine everyone for twenty-four days instead of fourteen? Besides, North Korea applies thirty days to ensure that there is no biphasic reaction.
6. What day are the facts going to come out that COVID-19 is a zoonotic Franken Germ?
7. How can there be a vaccine without a direct sample that passes the Kochs and Postulates test? Why is there SM 102 in one of the vaccines? Don't they know that its chloroform? This turns into phosgene gas when it breaks down, causing death parallel to COVID 18, 19, and the variants via the new COVID 21.
8. Why did China reject help from other nations and the WHO in order to bring things back under control and

normal? Why did they reject it? What happened to the protestors in Hong Kong? Were they erased? Are some of the protestors in the new hospitals that were built within ten days resemble that of group solitary confinement on steroids?

9. Why did Iran release 54,000 prisoners from its jails into society after 500 people had died? Will we see and hear more countries doing the same?
10. Did we miss the window of opportunity before it mutated? Why is that Mr. and Mrs. Gates are so upset on funding being halted to the WHO (worst health org), and will their version of the vaccine work? Without extra additives and preservatives like pages 2000 and 1510–1513 of HR 3990, otherwise called the (UN) Affordable Care Act, can this be done?
11. Italy has twenty-four separate strains from the first people who were reported infected. How do we know that this Franken Germ has not done the same over here in the USA, given that we do have two strains of this problem? Which is not reported? Are we, as a nation, hiding the truth or like being lied to by other leaders?
12. Nobody ever spoke on the long-term effects that stem from having contacted this Franken Germ, so why doesn't the military allow you to enlist once you have had it?
13. My personal suggestion is that everyone should have one of those asbestos-type suits in the stash with the boots and a few other oddities needed just in case. Use some of the money that is in the pipeline to get your house in *order*. Yes, I would seal the items in plastic and store them away in case of—and when the next attack comes. My gut feeling since this started has been *it's not over*!
14. Whatever agency and persons in the USA that led to the financing of this horrible germ and outsourcing it to China, will they be held, charged, and convicted for treason? Assets seized? What would happen to their families? If married, would the spouse or mistress be charged and investigated?

Children's Health Defense

NOTICE FOR EMPLOYERS, UNIVERSITIES AND OTHER INSTITUTIONS MANDATING COVID-19 TESTS

Revised 6/4/21

This serves as notice that the mandate for any individual to be tested against COVID-19 for employment or participation at a university or other institution violates federal law. All COVID-19 tests, whether polymerase chain reaction (PCR), antigen tests or others, are authorized, not approved or licensed, by the federal government; they are Emergency Use Authorization (EUA) only. They merely "may be effective." Federal law states:

Title 21 U.S.C. § 360bbb-3(e)(1)(A)(ii)(I-III) of the Federal Food, Drug, and Cosmetic Act states:

> **individuals to whom the product is administered are informed—**
> (I) that the Secretary has authorized the emergency use of the product;
> (II) of the significant known and potential benefits and risks of such use, and of the extent to which such benefits and risks are unknown; and
> **(III) of the option to accept or refuse administration of the product**, of the consequences, if any, of refusing administration of the product, and of the alternatives to the product that are available and of their benefits and risks.

EUA products are by definition experimental and thus require the right to refuse. Under the Nuremberg Code, the foundation of ethical medicine, no one may be coerced to participate in a medical experiment. Consent of the individual is "absolutely essential." A federal court held that even the U.S. military could not mandate EUA vaccines to soldiers. *Doe #1 v. Rumsfeld*, 297 F.Supp.2d 119 (2003).

The Food and Drug Administration (FDA) has issued Emergency Use Authorizations for over 200 different test kits manufactured by various organizations. Each of FDA's EUA letters relies on 21 U.S.C. § 360bbb-3(e)(1)(A)(ii)(I- III), stating: "This test is only authorized for the duration of the declaration that circumstances exist justifying the authorization of emergency use of in vitro diagnostics for detection and/or diagnosis of SARS-CoV-2...."

Liability for coercing participation in a medical experiment, and any injury from it, may be incalculable. Children's Health Defense urges U.S. employers, universities and other institutions to respect and uphold the rights of individuals to refuse EUA tests.

This notice is adapted from materials at Health Freedom Defense Fund, https://healthfreedomdefense.org/

1227 North Peachtree Parkway, Suite 202. Peachtree City, GA 30269
www.childrenshealthdefense.org

Children's Health Defense

NOTICE FOR EMPLOYERS, UNIVERSITIES AND OTHER INSTITUTIONS MANDATING COVID-19 MASKS

Revised 6/4/21

This serves as notice that the mandate for any individual to wear a mask against COVID-19 for employment or attendance at a university or other institution violates federal law. All COVID-19 masks, whether surgical, N95 or other respirators, are authorized, not approved or licensed, by the federal government; they are Emergency Use Authorization (EUA) only. They merely "may be effective." Federal law states:

Title 21 U.S.C. § 360bbb-3(e)(1)(A)(ii)(I-III) of the Federal Food, Drug, and Cosmetic Act (FD&C Act) states:

> **individuals to whom the product is administered are informed-**
> (I) that the Secretary has authorized the emergency use of the product;
> (II) of the significant known and potential benefits and risks of such use, and of the extent to which such benefits and risks are unknown; and
> **(III) of the option to accept or refuse administration of the product**, of the consequences, if any, of refusing administration of the product, and of the alternatives to the product that are available and of their benefits and risks.

EUA products are by definition experimental and thus require the right to refuse. Under the Nuremberg Code, the foundation of ethical medicine, no one may be coerced to participate in a medical experiment. Consent of the individual is "absolutely essential." A federal court held that even the U.S. military could not mandate EUA vaccines to soldiers. *Doe #1 v. Rumsfeld*, 297 F.Supp.2d 119 (2003).

In a letter dated April 24, 2020, the Food and Drug Administration stated that authorized face masks must be labelled accurately and may not be labeled in a way that misrepresents the product's intended use as "source control to help prevent the spread of SARS-CoV-2." The letter specifies that the labeling "may not state or imply that the product is intended for antimicrobial or antiviral protection or related uses or is for use such as infection prevention or reduction." Any EUA mandate requiring individuals to wear face masks conflicts with Section 360bbb-3(e)(1)(A)(ii)(I-III), which provides that the person must be informed of the option to refuse to wear the device.

Liability for forced participation in a medical experiment, including possible injury, may be incalculable. Children's Health Defense urges U.S. employers, universities and other institutions to respect and uphold the rights of individuals to refuse to wear EUA masks.

This notice is adapted from materials at Health Freedom Defense Fund, https://healthfreedomdefense.org/

1227 North Peachtree Parkway, Suite 202. Peachtree City, GA 30269
www.childrenshealthdefense.org

Children's Health Defense

NOTICE FOR EMPLOYERS, UNIVERSITIES AND OTHER INSTITUTIONS MANDATING COVID-19 VACCINES

Revised 6/4/21

This serves as notice that the requirement for any individual to be vaccinated against COVID-19 for employment or participation at a university or other institution violates federal law. All COVID-19 vaccines are merely authorized, not approved or licensed, by the federal government; they are Emergency Use Authorization (EUA) only. They merely "may be effective." Federal law states:

Title 21 U.S.C. § 360bbb-3(e)(1)(A)(ii)(I-III) of the Federal Food, Drug, and Cosmetic Act states:

> **individuals to whom the product is administered are informed—**
>
> (I) that the Secretary has authorized the emergency use of the product;
> (II) of the significant known and potential benefits and risks of such use, and of the extent to which such benefits and risks are unknown; and
> (III) **of the option to accept or refuse administration of the product**, of the consequences, if any, of refusing administration of the product, and of the alternatives to the product that are available and of their benefits and risks.

EUA products are by definition experimental and thus require the right to refuse. Under the Nuremberg Code, the foundation of ethical medicine, no one may be coerced to participate in a medical experiment. Consent of the individual is "absolutely essential." A federal court held that the U.S. military could not mandate EUA vaccines to soldiers. *Doe #1 v. Rumsfeld*, 297 F.Supp.2d 119 (2003). The court held: "...the United States cannot demand that members of the armed forces also serve as guinea pigs for experimental drugs." *Id.* at 135. No court has ever upheld a mandate for an EUA vaccine.

The liability for forced participation in a medical experiment, including injury or death, may be incalculable. Medical and religious exemptions will be insufficient to overcome the illegality of EUA vaccine mandates. Children's Health Defense urges U.S. employers, universities and other institutions to respect and uphold the rights of individuals to refuse EUA COVID-19 vaccines.

This notice is adapted from materials at Health Freedom Defense Fund, https://healthfreedomdefense.org/

1227 North Peachtree Parkway, Suite1 202. Peachtree City, GA 30269
www.childrenshealthdefense.org

Date

President _____________
University
Address
City-state-zip

Dear _____________,

I am greatly concerned about your plans for vaccination policy. It is my understanding that you are planning to update the Immunization Requirements for Students to include the COVID-19 vaccine.

Before you implement such a plan, I'd like you to consider that even though many university vaccination requirements for licensed and approved vaccines have been upheld in court, no court has ever upheld a mandate for an Emergency Use Authorization (EUA) vaccine, which all COVID vaccines are at present. In fact, a federal court has held that EUA vaccines cannot be mandated to soldiers in the U.S. military, who enjoy far fewer rights than civilians, *Doe #1 u. Rumsfeld*, 297 F.Supp.2d 119 (2003). That court remarkably held "....the United States cannot demand that members of the armed forces also serve as guinea pigs for experimental drugs." Id. at 135.

Federal law 21 U.S.C. § 360bbb-3(e)(1)(A)(ii)(III) requires that the person to whom an EUA vaccine is administered be advised, "of the option to accept **or refuse** administration of the product, of the consequences, if any, of refusing administration ofthe product, and of the alternatives to the product that are available and of their benefits and risks." The reason for the right of refusal stems from the fact that EUA products are by definition experimental. Under the Nuremberg Code, no one may be coerced to participate in a medical experiment. Consent of the individual is "absolutely essential." The liability for forced participation in a medical experiment, not to mention injury from such coerced medical intervention, may be incalculable. The consequences described in the statute mean medical consequences, not termination of employment or denial of in-person learning, as Rutgers contemplates.

Children's Health Defense (CHD) and Robert F. Kennedy, Jr. have recently filed civil complaints on behalf of citizens regarding EUA products. They have also filed an FDA petition to revoke EUA COVID vaccines and refrain from approving and licensing them. The FDA petition was imperative as our government health agencies continue to ignore the astonishing numbers of deaths and injuries being reported to the U.S. Health and Human Services (HHS) Vaccine Adverse Events Reporting System (VAERS). Updated each Friday, the May 21 data release reports 227,805 adverse events and 4201 deaths following vaccination with COVID-19 vaccines from mid-December, 2020 through May 14, 2021. Alarmingly, a 2010 HHS study found that less than 1% of adverse events are ever reported to VAERS. Despite this, government agencies at local, state and national levels continue to promote uptake of these vaccines.

The research is growing every day that COVID-19 vaccines are not necessary and can be very harmful, especially to young people. It is my sincere hope that you will reconsider your decision in light of the above facts.

Sincerely,

____

P.S. Also please see the document: Notice for employers, universities and other institutions mandating COVID-19 vaccines.

Advocacy

- Preventing Vaccine Mandates Toolkit
- Detailed Longer Letter to School Districts or Universities
- Shorter COVID-19 Vaccine Mandate Letter for Colleges
- 50-state Update on Pending Legislation Pertaining to Employer-mandated Vaccinations

Epilogue

Thank you for purchasing this book, and I hope that a lot of the practices and preparations give you a standing to excellence. A lot of the things presented are for you to practice, because it has helped me in my current walk with Jesus Christ. There are many times that I have prayed, and God has heard my petitions and has brought forth some things of change for the better. Even when I was in my first year in college, majoring in Paralegal Studies and Business Administration, to later on transfer to a senior college to major in Political Science and Social Work, I prayed for all my teachers and professors as well as those that they have to answer to. It has helped me and it was not easy during that time. Because when truth needed to be set forth, it could not sit in my gut without the word being stated in an open class. Well, for many classes where we had to brief cases, some of the cases were briefed according to the standard of the Bible. Now, professors did not know it at first, until they had to look at the "Table of Authorities," which is just like the table of contents in a regular book.

However, how can you live in the United States of America and not realize that the historical bonding of our laws comes from the Bible (most of them)? Professors have tried to argue it and stated it was religion. Yet in all, there is no separation of church and state when the church is in the jurisdiction of the state, just like there are three sides of a quarter. It was the simplicity of the history that was overlooked and one thing that remains true. When you do not pay attention to the past, you are bound to repeat similar behaviors in the present. They agreed, and that was the end of the challenges of using law combined with scripture from the Bible. For many have their own personal hang-ups about the Bible, and it is a book of finances, history, archeology, biology, culture, and the truth of the first time the languages of the earth came forth. Many try to argue it, and yet they all see and find out later that it all traces back to the time when the Tower of Babel was being built in Babylon,[43] [44]located off Mesopotamia. The rest is in the book of Genesis. The funny thing is, America exercises the same things as the former Roman Empire, but for those who take heed as to what is going on, you will not be shocked but will be very aware.

It is my understanding that even under the freedom of religion, we as a people still have a freedom of speech. That is and shall not be abrogated by any man or woman.

We have to stay vigilant in prayer and have supplies as a people. So, everyone, there is one thing that we need to do. Stack up on some mask. For the smart virus, the following masks are suggested: N95, N99 N100, 3M 6200, 7500, and 2091.[45] And another thing is, about 80% of our generic medicines and penicillin are made in China, so do whatever you can to stay healthy. If people think of it as crazy and don't care to practice some level of social distancing with folks that

---

[43] There is an ancient city in Mesopotamia, which is the capital of Babylonia from the period of the second millennium BC. The city was on the banks of the Euphrates River and was noted for its luxury, its fortifications, and particularly, for the Hanging Gardens of Babylon.

[44] Legendary terraced gardens at Babylon watered by pumps from the Euphrates, whose construction was ascribed to Nebuchadnezzar (c. 600 BC). It is one of the Seven Wonders of the Ancient World.

[45] I found out that in order to get around the waiting period, use N99, N100, washable and reusable mask or FFP3 and 3M-8210, the mask 3M-6200 respirator masks, and just buy filters. Lastly, buy gloves by the case. Some may say that it's hoarding, especially when they cannot afford to buy them and you're hooking your family up first! I learned that most of the haters usually are the ones that cannot afford or do not have the funds to purchase what you did for you and your family. Keep in mind that as time goes on, keep a respirator mask with eye coverage in the stash too (just in case, things get worse; I pray that it doesn't). The last thing they are going to release is a killer waive again, and we need to be prepared. We have some time before the death angel walks the land again in September through November, which, according to my sources, is next year. And we are about to get it on with Iran. The suitcase nukes that was discussed in *Really???* I pray that the Lord Jesus will send his angels to assist the first responders and others to find and disarm without any casualties or damage to property in Jesus's Name. Amen.

are not from within the same household as you, then it can challenging. We must keep in mind that from my knowledge of this plague, we should have pets tested as well—from goldfish to your grandfather's pet giraffe—just to be on the safe side and for this not to come back again in a more deadly strain. Stay prayerful and remember the update about the truckers in the later page is based on a timeline of what you have to do before the trucks stop bringing supplies to your town. The truckers are the heroes that keep cities from tearing themselves apart, with the many new guidelines that affect food delivery. One main rule is that if you drive through New York State, you must stay quarantined for fourteen days. Many truckers can grow weary of this process, so we all need to thank God for the men, women, and families that drive trucks for our every need to come through. Thank them and show your support for the other forgotten essential workers—the truckers. That is why this portion of love was written for you to realize they matter too!

Warning: 2021 onward, bad things are going to come, prepare your prayer closet. Also, remember history repeats itself, and for that, bear in mind all the events that happened and continue to stack and stash the necessary items which you will need. A lot of serious details are being finalized for later on.

References

American Trucking Association. 2015. "When Trucks Stop, America Stops: A Timeline Showing the Deterioration of Major Industries Following a Truck Stoppage."

Benjamin Fulford. 2020. "Engineered Novel Coronavirus Okay for Europeans."

"Bulletin: Testicular Cells Are the Potential Targets of 2019 nCoV." Aired February 15, 2020. Hal Turner Radio.

Channel 4 News (English Subtitles). Aired February 17, 2020. YouTube.

Conspiracy. Episode 3. Cultivation 5. Dated: unknown

"Control by Funimation." www.funimation.com.

"Coronavirus: Fears of Two-Phase Infections as Recovered Japan Patient Tests Positive." Aired 2020. New Zealand Radio.

"COVID-19: What You're Not Being Told by Officials or Media: This will Be Survival of the Fittest. The Rest will Die." Aired February 27, 2020. HalTurnerRadioShow.com.

David Wilkerson. 1998. *God's Plan to Protect His People in the Coming Depression.* Wilkerson Trust Publications.

Dr. Leroy Thompson Sr. 1999. *Money Thou Art Loosed.*

Eyewitness News. Aired March 11, 2020. WABC-Channel 7.

"Food Shortage Warning for 2019." YouTube.

Gloria Copeland. 2012. *Living the Dream.*

Good Morning America. Featuring Barbara Corcoran. Aired March 21, 2020. WABC-TV. New York.

HR 4827. "Killing of the Dollar." 2014

HR 835 Section 3

HR 3990 and page 1510–1513 speak on chipping (not your pet) and page 2000

How North Korea Is Reporting on Coronavirus (English Subtitles). Aired February 17, 2020.

Jessie Duplantis Ministries. 2015. "Let's Us Pray." Revised by Jabbar. 2019.

John Copeland. "Prospering in a World of Cycles."

2019. "KCM Letter."

Marilyn Hickey Ministries. 2019. "The War on Debt." *Letter on Mark 12:41–44.*

"Proof: The Novel Coronavirus Infecting the World Is a Military Bioweapon Developed by China's Army." Aired February 1, 2020. Hal Turner Radio.

"The Coronavirus Is Killing Far More Men than Women." www.thehour.com.

The Holy Bible. AMP, Classic Edition.

The Holy Bible. King James Version.

"This Week: Medical Collapse, Food Shortage, and Anarchy, Begin." www.halturnerradioshow.com.

Tim Macwelch and the editors of *Outdoor Life.* 2015, 2016, 2017. "Prepare for Anything Survival Manual." *Outdoor Life.*

"Two Strains of Coronavirus!" Aired March 4, 2020. www.halturnerradioshow.com.

"Update: France and Czech Republic Halts the Sale of Masks to the General Public; Only Healthcare Workers." Aired March 4, 2020.

Webster's Dictionary. Collegiate 9th Edition.

WION. "America Import by Chinese Spies." Aired March 18, 2020. YouTube.

Places for Help

CORONAVIRUSNOW.COM
www.NY.GOV/CORONAVIRUS

Our thoughts and prayers to those survivors of this Franken Germ, and my condolences for those who lost loved ones in the battle of life to COVID-19.

Also, see the three positives from the coronavirus from Motivating You to Win on YouTube, aired March 12, 2020, and I found the information to help those in need of such. God bless you and may Jesus Christ bless America!

Pray this prayer to join the winning team and prepare your new life to ball out in heaven, where the streets are paved with gold and never need servicing or experience damage from the elements.

> Dear God,
>
> I am a sinner and need forgiveness. I believe that Jesus Christ shed his precious blood and died for my sins. I am willing to turn from sin. I now invite Christ to come into my heart as my personal savior. Amen.

For orders of autographed books and other information, contact Jabbar, @Jabbarthewatch1 on Twitter or type the hashtags #NEEDACURE, #FREEUSSOON, #PRAY4US, or #PSALM23.

Please be advised that Ann Tracts Ministries is now owned by Jabbar Enterprises LLC. Check with us about the selection of tracts.

Coming soon:

God Has a Plan for Me and I Am Willing to Wait

Really??? The Amendment (Featuring the following)

What You Do Eat Matters! And *Gold Digger "Christians."* Find out who lead the change on believing that populace should have abortions instead of having babies applying language like "concerns of population growth and particularly growth in populations that we don't want to have too many of." Some things will surprise you, including topics on sperm tax, is your bank under a RICO investigation, and more.

Three hundred and twenty-one years to go before the millennium reign.

Many prophecies were spoken, many were fulfilled in our faces, and there are more to come. How Matthew 24, Luke 21, and Mark 13 are overlooked. The Bible being ignored and used as a paperweight, and the coming of the third beast with the wings of the fowl.

About the Author

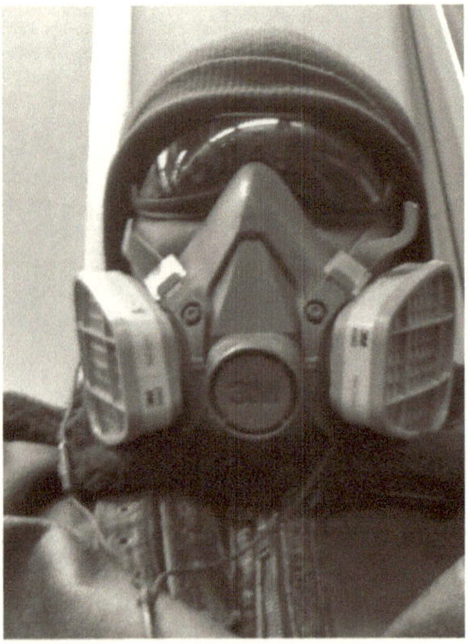

The Author is a man that believes in finances. And the lack thereof breeds problems yet in all with a mentor or two Jabbar brings love plus jokes in the release.

www.ingramcontent.com/pod-product-compliance
Lightning Source LLC
Chambersburg PA
CBHW031048180526
45163CB00002BA/735
9781638746706